The Quill Pen

PARAKALAMA
The Quill Pen

Performed at the National Drama Festival
at Delhi in 1954, as the best Odia play.

Gopal Chhotray

Translated by
Prafulla Kumar Mohanty

BLACK EAGLE BOOKS
2021

BLACK EAGLE BOOKS

USA address:
7464 Wisdom Lane
Dublin, OH 43016

India address:
E/312, Trident Galaxy, Kalinga Nagar,
Bhubaneswar-751003, Odisha, India

E-mail: info@blackeaglebooks.org
Website: www.blackeaglebooks.org

First Published in 1955
by N.L.Gupta of Janashakti Pustakalaya
Binod Bihari, Cuttack-2

First International Edition Published by
BLACK EAGLE BOOKS, 2021

THE QUILL PEN
Original by Gopal Chhotray
Translated by **Prafulla Kumar Mohanty**

Copyright © **Gopal Chhotray Foundation Trust**
Translation Copyright © **Prafulla Kumar Mohanty**

All rights reserved. No part of this publication may be reproduced, stored in a retrieval system, or transmitted, in any form or by any means, electronic, mechanical, photocopying, recording or otherwise without the prior permission of the publisher.

Cover & Interior Design: Ezy's Publication

ISBN- 978-1-64560-147-0 (Paperback)
Library of Congress Control Number: 2021930592

Printed in United States of America

for
Babu & Jhunu

PARAKALAMA
Janata Theatre
Banka Bazaar, Cuttack

First Performance
5 August 1954, evening

Cast
Acharya - Niranjan
Rajendra - Bholanath
Mahapatra – Balai Babu
Sharma – Kartik
Debananda – Rushyashrunga
Mandara – Benudhara
Makunda – Tima
Radhu – Brundaban
Satyabadi – Prafulla
Sapana – Sharat Mohanty
Bijay – Ajeet
Sashi – Nata
Geeta – Umasashi
Sita – Purnachandra
Seba – Krushnamani
Surama – Anuradha

Singer of the song 'Dayi kiye' - Sarat Satpathy
In other dance & song sequence – Sarat, Prabhuram, Sudha,
Aniruddha, Chakradhar, Kumud & Anuradha, etc.

Director – Niranjan Satpathy
Assistant Director – Bholanath Das
Song Composition and Music – Kishore Kabi Shyam Sundar Das
Choreography – Mayadhara Raut
Music Lesson – Prabhakar Padhi
Prompter – Prafulla & Sarat

Musical Instruments – Prabhakar, Prabhuram, Benu, Sudhir,
Baishnab and Radhanath

A play like 'Parakalama' can give lessons to many politicians and even to the members of the Cabinet.

Harekrushna Mahatab
Chief Minister of Odisha

Preface

A couple of years back, I had read out to a well known theatre director the synopsis of the story of 'Parakalama' and sought his views. While listening, he started knitting his brows. That a completely political play has no place in professional theatre constituted his anxiety. It is also curious that till the last moment before the play went on to the stage, persons connected with it were doubtful about its commercial success.

'Parakalama' was released on 5 August 1954 in Janata Theatre in the presence of Dr Harekrushna Mahatab, the Chief Minister of Odisha. Its success went on to prove that political plays have a place in the precincts of commercial theatre. I have nothing more to add.

I am grateful to the management of the Janata Theatre, the director of the play, and the actors and actresses for staging this play with courage and forbearance.

Kaligali **Gopal Chhotray**
Cuttack-2
2 September 1954

Press Clipings

This play, centered around party based election and unprincipled exercise of power, was immensely enjoyable. Above all, the actors and their craft and skill made this drama elegant and lively.

Matrubhumi, 7.8.54

Earlier to this, Mr Chhotray's 'Bharasa' enacted on the same stage had secured a very special place in the theatres of Odisha.
    The structure of climax and catastrophe in the play has enhanced its success. Writing of such a play denotes a new contribution to the body of Odia dramatic literature. Acting of characters as Mandar Mohanty, Education Minister, Seba Bou and Sapana is noteworthy.

Samaja, 7.8.54

'Prakalama' is a play, dealing with the new political critique. It is indeed great that 'Parakalama' dislodged the mores of traditional theatre, which the commercial stages of Odisha were used to abide by. The writer has been able to capture with biting humour, through characters and situations, the crooked and corrupt practices that had entered into the contemporary Indian politics after Independence.

Krushak, 9.8.54

This is the first instance of a play of this nature being enacted on a commercial stage in Odisha. It is heartening that the writer has hit at the roots of the traditional, unreal and reactive thinking. Ordinarily the litterateurs perceive that politics has no place in literature. It's another way of saying, by the so called practioners of literature, that general public do not participate in politics. Such a perception is wrong and reactionary. If all parts of life and activities in their totality are not truly reflected by the writers, that would amount to narrow down literature. Then it would be conceived as the flights of imagination of a few. The efforts of Gopal Chhotray deserves rich commendation as much as the proprietors of Janata Theatres.

Nua Dunia, 12.08.54

In the state of Odisha, only one playwright, Sri Gopal Chhotray, has the daring of writing a play on a political subject, and have it enacted it in the precincts of a professional theatre.
    Since the playwright has delved into the electoral politics as a part of the system, after India became a Republic, the play therefore reflects the necessary contemporaneity. Since the dialogues are crafted in simple language, it is hoped that the common man will able to learn a lot about the democratic process.

Prajatantra, 29.08.1954

A Word from the Translator

Prafulla Kumar Mohanty

In Post-Independence Odia drama Gopal Chotroy's *Para Kalam*(The Quill Pen) is a turning point for it introduced for the first time a kind of expressionist technique to externalize the psychic conflict of the hero. *Para Kalam* is the first political drama in Odia literature. The play amalgamates the rural and urban into a new whole where the changing face of Odia culture almost settles into a new found modernity. The characterization is realistic with several levels of Odia consciousness. A new hope for life in the partially understood democratic values elevates the political theme to a sharpened sense of morality. The dramatist is a conscious reformist trying to give politics a moral purity.

Gopal Chotroy was a prolific writer and almost all his plays seem to have a Gandhian approach updated by a modernist sophistication. Progress not at the cost of moral compromise, is Chotroy's writerly credo. But there is no preaching or authorial interference; the play is pure theatre and the characters are not mouthpieces of the dramatist's ideological leanings. It is and will remain in the history of Odia drama as a literary signpost. As drama *Para Kalam* can still enthrall the contemporary audience.

I enjoyed translating this masterpiece. I had watched the performance of this play at Berhampur when I was a young man and I was delighted to translate it when Devdas requested me. I have left out the songs because the images in the songs may not have any appeal to modern audience. But if a present day director wishes to have them he can use other songs as in Epic theatre to highlight a contrastive experience.

I will feel rewarded if Gopal Chotroy's play in English translation is enjoyed by the post covid generations.

Chtrakabya, Sishu Bihar,
Bhubaneswar-751024
Kartik Purnima
30 November 2020

Act I : Scene – i

(The State Assembly Hall. The Session is on. In the Visitors' Gallery, among others is a young woman, about 20/21 years of age. When the scene begins the audience sees the Leader of the Opposition Sri Ramanarayan Acharjya on his feet)

Acharjya: Today is the last day of this session. After this session is over the Assembly will be dissolved. The election is after two months. The present Government's time will end after two months. The people will vote for a new Government. In this situation – I don't understand – why this farce is going on here.

Sharma: I draw the kind attention of the Hon'ble Speaker to the speech made by the leader of Opposition. He has used 'Farce' in his speech. This is in my view unparliamentary – I take serious objection to it.

Debanand: We are not bound to accept your view.

Sharma: You will be compelled to accept – this word reduces the dignity of the House.

Rajendra: Why is 'Farce' objectionable ? The honourable representative of Nuapatna may kindly explain.

Sharma: It is true that the word *Farce* has come from English. But it has almost been naturalized into Odia. Farce means a ridiculous comic

	episode, a *tamasa* normally associated with Jatra Parties. Yet the leader of Opposition describes the proceedings of the House as farce – this is strange. I hope the honourable member will apologize and withdraw the word.

Acharjya: No ! I have deliberately used this word in the present contest. Not only today – what the Ganasakti Party has done since the day they assumed power – if you consider all those, Farce is the only appropriate word.

Sharma: Well then, I urge the honourable Speaker's view.

Speaker: Whether the word is objectionable or not. I will give my ruling later.

Sharma: Thank you.

Acharjya: The appropriate bills which this Government is getting passed in the name of Supplementary Budget, how was it urgently required ? The only answer to this question is – vote. The elections are knocking at the door. The regions and constituencies for which the Ganasakti Party expects maximum votes, only in those areas this money will be spent. I will call this system a vote – buying system. But by doing this the Ganasakti Party is digging its own grave - this they must understand. *(Sits down)*.

Sharma: If we're digging our own graves the Opposition should breathe in peace, why does Mr. Acharjya worry over it ? But his logic is skewed. Elections are near, therefore all people friendly measures should come to a grinding halt ? People will not drink clean water, will not walk on roads ? Will not seek treatment of diseases !!! Strange is this allegation. All these measures are not done properly – was the war cry of the opposition here, in this house, the other day. Yet today the allegation is only to buy votes Government is proposing to make wells, tanks and roads ? They wouldn't have accused us if they had considered the matter from another perspective. Why have we come here empowered by votes ? The opposition perhaps came here to quarrel with us on all issues but we have come to serve the people. We'll do that – come what may – If the Opposition raises objections only to stop us from doing things for the people, then the grave which Mr. Acharjya was referring to, the Opposition members I fear will fall into it – not us. *(Sits down accompanied by the cheers of the Treasury Bench).*

Rajendra: Mr. Sharma, member of the ruling party said that he has been voted to serve the people. Good ! But had this serving instinct been his motive five years ago, that is, since the day they formed the Government, we wouldn't have been quarrelling here like this. *(Hear ! Hear ! from the Opposition benches).*

Sharma: No, no such chance.

Rajendra: I know, the ministers won't resign because they want to visit their constituencies for campaign work by taking Government

	money. Government had not yet given the commitment that during elections all parties will be given equal scope and opportunities.
Mohapatra:	I give you my word of honour as Chief Minister – all parties will get equal scope and opportunity in this election campaign. *(Applause from the Treasury Bench).*
Rajendra:	I thank Chief Minister Sri Mohapatra for this, but one more thing – all know that in respect of food grains Odisha is a surplus state. We supply to other states but what's happening here ? At the slightest indication bags of superfine rice stack up at the feet of our bureaucrats and power brokers – where as for a Kg of sand, stone mixed ordinary rice people break heads in our markets. We have enough rice to sustain people but people die of starvation. Why this anomaly. I declare on behalf of my Party, that is the United Party, we'll fight this election on this food policy of the Government. This is our challenge to the Ganasakti Party. *(from the Opposition Benches there was applause – a woman sitting in the visitor's gallery joined that applause. Suddenly she became conscious that the attention of the House is on her. She somewhat shrank and her applause automatically stopped. Looking bashfully at Rajendra for a while she sat with her head downcast. Rajendra too sat down).*
Mohapatra:	Whatever discussion happened in the House from that I have clearly understood that the hon'ble members of the House are more

interested in the coming elections than in the agenda of the House. This discussion will gain more heat during elections but the discussion would have one main focus – 'Whom to vote and whom not to' – but why to this Party. I firmly believe our voters do not have the analytical mind to stress 'Why' and to scrutinize the issues involved. Therefore, instead of promising heaven to them in return of their votes if we can explain the meaning and significance of election to them, I trust, the purpose of democracy will be better served. *(Applause)*. The hon'ble Deputy Leader of Opposition Sri Rajendranath Das is a young man – he has already proved that his blood is always at a boiling point.

Acharjya: Only at 22 Pitt could be the Prime Minister of England. Our Deputy Leader, my friend Rajendra is a young man – but the Chief Minister should not attack him on his righteousness.

Sharma: I entirely agree with the hon'ble member from the Opposition. In this context I recall two lines of poetry.
'He is not old who's grey at the top
He who devotes his youth to knowledge
Let him be an Assembly Member'
(Laughter)

Debanand: *(Waking up from dozing)* Hon'ble member is now reciting poetry. I'm afraid one day he may arrange song and dance programmes here.

Sharma: Hon'ble member was dozing while sitting here. I'm afraid one day he will come here with a canvas cot and pillows and may arrange to sleep here.

(Laughter)

Mohapatra: Young Rajendra Babu has complained that Govt's Food Policy is wayward. Our State is surplus State – yet people die here of starvation. I've many a times answered this issue in this House. He has challenged us to fight the next election on this issue, but he forgets that this is not a common meeting on the Municipal grounds, this is the House of the Assembly. I won't reply to his challenge here; but let me assure him that at the proper place and time he will get the right reply. (*Hear hear from Treasury Bench*).

Speaker: The Leader of Opposition in his speech had used the word Farce. In my view the word is objectionable. The word will not find place in the Assembly Records.

Now, I would like to inform the Hon'ble Members that we have now only an hour – you know that after this sitting the Assembly will be dissolved. I, therefore request all members to kindly pay attention to all items on agenda during this one hour.

■

Act I : Scene –ii

(The Lobby adjacent to the House. The Assembly session is over – members and other officers are going out – time 5.00 PM. Rajendra appears after some time. Pulled out a cigarette from the case and lit it – his expression betrayed some kind of waiting for some one...... enters Sharma)

Rajendra:	Please come Sir …..
Sharma:	Cigarette ! Thanks. The trade mark of our Party is cigar but cigar was so strong that it could not match the liberal policy of Ganasakti Party. That's why we are compelled to smoke cigarettes.
Rajendra:	Your sense of humour is quite appetizing.
Sharma:	I saw some members weep for the Assembly now stands dissolved.
Rajendra:	They are definitely members of your party.
Sharma:	Why ? Didn't your Party members not take their salary or were not invited to Tea parties and Dinner programmes ?
Rajendra:	Oh ! The reason for their tears is this ?
Sharma:	If the Puri temple crashes down I doubt if any one will ever shed tears – why should they cry because the Assembly is dissolved? Come, let's have tea.
Rajendra:	Excuse me…..
Sharma:	Oh ! Waiting…. Ok tell me what's the news?

Rajendra: Tell me about yourself first.

Sharma: My news ? After getting a Law degree when I didn't practice and entered politics at that time I had 60 acres of land. In my 19 years of political life I have sold 8 acres. Tomorrow I'll go home sell 2 more acres which will be a celebration of my 20th year in politics. Then I'll come to the medical with my wife. Her jaundice has become acute. The eldest son has passed I.Sc. in 1st Division, now the problem is whether he would go for medicine, engineering or B.Sc. – the youngest son after failing Matric will be a socialist or communist or Mess Manager in the Congress Ashram is another problem. Daughters haven't married and I don't think they can marry.

Rajendra: Why ?

Sharma: I can't give dowry to a professional groom. The unemployed candidates want their M.L.A. would be father-in-law, should arrange jobs for them and they will marry later. Whereas the rules of our Party.......

Rajendra: Do all members of your Party follow rules ?

Sharma: Those who sell two acres of land every year they certainly follow rules.

(Enters Gita. Gita is that girl who clapped from the visitor's gallery while Rajendra was speaking).

Gita: Good evening uncle...... you !

Sharma: Rajendra is waiting for you alone – I gossiped with him to while away time. Ok – let me go

Gita:	Bah ! Why should you go ? Please stay.
Sharma:	My dear ! Rajendra Babu is waiting for you, not me.
Gita:	Are you going home ?
Sharma:	After I come back from the canteen (*goes*).
Rajendra:	Have you met with your father ?
Gita:	No.
Rajendra:	Your passionate applause after my speech has given scope to many to think of many things.
Gita:	Really, it was a mistake.
Rajendra:	You must have noticed, the attention of the whole Assembly was on you.
Gita:	What choice did I have ? Clapping was under my control. But the indomitable urge to clap, does it wait for another's control ? (*She was bashful automatically after speaking*).
Rajendra:	Exactly at such moments perhaps politics becomes enjoyable for a male ! (*Suddenly but regretfully Gita looked at Rajendra and moved her eyes away*) Here comes your father ! (*Gita became normal and waited and almost at the same time entered Chief Minister Mohapatra. Gita is his daughter. After going ahead crossing her he paused...... Gita too advanced towards him*).
Mohapatra:	Are you going home ?
Gita:	Yes.
Mohapatra:	Will you go with me in the car ?
Gita:	Yes, let's go. (*Mohapatra left. Gita turned back and looked at Rajendra – Rajendra indicated a silent goodbye, Gita walked away – while Rajendra was undecided what to do, entered Sharma*).

The Quill Pen | 23

Rajendra:	Had your tea ?
Sharma:	Like the crossing of the Oval market you are still standing here since then and after taking rounds I'm here !
Rajendra:	Let's go.
Sharma:	Can you write an essay comparing the lead singers of a Pala competition, the advocates of the two litigant parties and the leaders of two parties opposing each other ?
Rajendra:	*(laughing)* Why do such things come to your head ?
Sharma:	About after a fortnight both our parties will enter the vote arena for a bitter fight, at that time in the rallies what you will speak about us and what we will speak about you, rehearsing those things in your mind, come – we'll go together – the journey will be pleasant. *(pause)* Has Gita left ?
Rajendra:	Yes.
Sharma:	With her father ……. ?
Rajendra:	Yes – she is quite intimate to you – no ?
Sharma:	Yes intimate – although the relationship is purely political.
Rajendra:	Political ?
Sharma:	When in the beginning, I joined politics Gita's father, at that time was a top ranking Government Officer. By his kindness at that time I was sent to serve a six month term in the Uncle's House (Jail) true, but I didn't have the good luck of being Gita's uncle. Thereafter Mr. Mohapatra quit his job and joined our Party. Our relationship became political and I became Gita's Political uncle. Well, this time

	our symbol is Umbrella. What's yours ?
Rajendra:	Entirely new – Quill Pen.
Sharma:	Quill Pen ! Hereafter you will give up your own pen ? Quill Pen ! Fine.

■

Act I : Scene –iii

(Room in the Chief Minister's residence. He is speaking over the phone).

Mohapatra:	Yes now ! Any objection to coming here ? …. Ok… I will wait…. Come immediately. *(Kept the phone on the cradle but the hand was on it. That he was worried was evident from the face but his worry was not clearly visible on his face. Gita came ……. An open letter in her hand).*
Gita:	Father !
Mohapatra:	Who has sent the letter ?
Gita:	Come from the village.
Mohapatra:	Kulamani has written ?
Gita:	Yes.
Mohapatra:	The same old things or anything new ?
Gita:	Yes he has written ……. The middle portion of the house is almost in ruins – not a grain of paddy is collected from the share croppers….
Mohapatra:	*(Cutting her)* I know must have written many such things. He thinks you can sort out these things. That's why he writes to you, today also he has given. Why speak to me all these ?
Gita:	He's written to you too.

Mohapatra:	What, read.
Gita:	*(Reads)* I beg of you my child, please convince your father. I'm just a clerk, a servant, who listens to me ? Here everything is getting lost. If he wishes, he could set everything right. He manages the affairs of a big state can't he manage one house ? .... *(Mohapatra burst out laughing).*
Mohapatra:	Yes he has written the basic truth. Accha. My dear what is your idea about it ? *(Gita looked at him questioningly)* I am unfit to manage my house. In other words I've no authority in my house, no administration..........
Gita:	Administration !
Mohapatra:	First thing – What's the meaning of my worldly affairs ? My land, house and property – I haven't earned that. One day or other those things will slip away from my hand – if it goes today, so be it, why should I be unhappy ? Then what remains ?
Gita:	I know father – then I remain – your only daughter. Your world moves around me. Yet you have no authority on me – no control.
Mohapatra:	No point in suppressing the main issue, Gita. That day, after Rajendra's speech in the Assembly, the way you behaved – that has caused this situation between you and me.
Gita:	I admit, I'm at fault.
Mohapatra:	But if I blame you, in the public eye I'll be proved guilty. *(Gita looked questioningly at him)* People know, I'm a leader of this country, -

	the Chief Minister of a State. My policy is to give chance and opportunity to everyman to express his view freely….. But how can I explain this to anyone…. How to explain that the moment my twenty one year old daughter opens up her mind, my mind revolts against her… my heart and soul get agitated to exercise the natural control of a father on her and to make her stand before me with head downcast……
Gita:	I say again, father, I've done wrong.
Mohapatra:	But who will pronounce the judgment – that you are guilty ?
Gita:	My guilt does not wait for someone's decision or judgment. Many in the state support the United Party. Many are fans of Rajendra babu; but that day the Press went overboard in my praise because I supported him. Why ? Because, I'm your daughter, I am the daughter of the Chief Minister. Under the protection of your clout, exploiting your fame and prestige, I have given the garland of victory in your enemy's neck. Although I have chosen this path utilizing my intelligence and conscience, I understand, that to gain cheap popularity I have gone through the black market. This guilt is limitless, father ! But my last request father, please bear with me for three days.
Mohapatra:	No. *(Gita looked apprehensively).* I know, after three days you will choose a certain path. At that time, may be. I may not have the authority to admonish you as your

	father. Therefore, today only. I wish to exercise all my fatherly powers on you. Tell me, will you accept my authority ?
Gita:	I have given my answer.
Mohapatra:	Well then, I want …….. your marriage.
Gita:	Father !
Mohapatra:	Just this much I want Gita ………. Just this much will give me back all my fatherly dues.
Gita:	I am ready father, I will marry.
Mohapatra:	But whom to marry, that decision *(Here Gita's face lost all colours in apprehension)*, You'll take my child…… tell me what's in your mind ? Who do you want to marry ? *(Gita was silent. Face down she was drawing lines on the ground with her toe nails)* Ok, let me tell you what's in your mind, you will marry…… Rajendra ! *(Gita's heart beat increased. Slowly she lifted her face up).*
Gita:	Can I stand this test, father !
Mohapatra:	You can. I've telephoned Rajendra, must be coming.
Gita:	Why do you make this sacrifice for my sake ? I may not be free of this debt for lives together. *(Tears came into her eyes. The door bell rang).*
Mohapatra:	Who ? *(Sliding the curtains)* O' Rajendra ! Come in. *(Rajendra entered, paid his respects. Mohapatra in the meantime was normal)* Without any introduction let me straight come to the subject…. I want you to marry Gita. Gita has given her consent. Only your consent –
Rajendra:	So soon such a decision…….

Mohapatra:	No, not so soon, I have taken this decision earlier. Today I've communicated only.
Rajendra:	But the election is so near -
Mohapatra:	Therefore, this marriage must be solemnized very soon. After five days only.... Tell me what's your wish ?.... What are you thinking ? Permission of your Party ? Permission of Mr. Acharjya ?
Rajendra:	Why do you think, I am so weak ?
Mohapatra:	Then, you have no objection.
Rajendra:	No – I agree.
Mohapatra:	(*Heaves a sigh of relief*) Today I feel the matter deep in my heart. May God bless you. (*Leaves without giving them scope to speak anything*).
Gita:	(*emotionally choked*) What is this Rajendra babu ! Why this decision so suddenly ? How could you agree ? And how could I agree ! I don't understand anything. In fact was there any need for our marriage ?
Rajendra:	Yes, there was. Look back to the past, Gita. The attraction which brings man and woman together, we are no exception to that. Politics was the field of our union, but that the union was possible only because of love, none of us can ever deny. For the fruition of that love this marriage was necessary. That's why we must accept with bowed heads the decision of your father.

■

Act I : Scene –iv

(A road scene of a village. A group of workers was advancing singing a chorus. Every one was holding a Quill Pen. They were supporters of the United Party. At the head of the rally was a young man, Bijoy)
Song
(After the song Radhu Pani was walking that way)

Makunda: (from the wings) Hey ! Hey !
(Radhu walked on as if he didn't hear, as if he was trying to slip away)
Hey Radhu Pani ! *(Radhu paused unwillingly. Entered Makunda)*
Hey you ! In the shop, seeing me, you covered your face with your dhoti and walked away fast ! Is it not ?
Radhu: Why should I cover my face and slip away?
Makunda: I called you at the top of my voice, you couldn't hear ?
Radhu: Why did you call me ?
Makunda: Well listen to this fellow ! It's now more than one and half months. You don't bother to pay back the money you owe me – like the ground lizard, saying tomorrow – tomorrow you have shown me a world of tomorrows ! The vote people have spread over all villages. During this time I must collect money from

	here and there and set up a shop.. or you will be throwing tomorrow at me and I shall be behind you. Shell down my money, now.
Radhu:	(*angrily*) Makunda…..
Makunda:	O' what a temper !!
Radhu:	Would I not devalue your clout ! You small man – blocking my path at village road you will give me warning ? You're showing me money, money ? You dirty little man….. (*proudly goes away*).
Makunda:	See, do you see this fellow ! Well, wait, I will skin off your hauteur.

■

Act I : Scene – v

(Village. The court yard of Mandara Mohanty, 50 + stylish curled dhoti, closed neck half shirt. 19th century hair style – a long vermillion mark on the forehead, aristocratic moustache. After lunch he came belching. A pair of wooden slippers. A small mat under his armpit – a small contraption for paan making – Spreading the mat carefully he sat and made paan – and intermittent belching was going on)

Mandara: Seba's mother ! O' Seba's mother !
Sita: *(from inside)* What ?
(After a while Seba bou, i.e. his wife Sita enters, She stood there. Mohanty looked at her with pleasing eyes)
Mandara: You 've come ! …. Sit …
(Sita was going away making a face)
Seba's mother …. Come. I say, Sit sit. *(Sita sat unwillingly).*
O' what a hand ! you 've got a hand ! You have given me the taste of ambrosia. Worm – infested horsegram of what age ! That dal could be so tasty ! Nah ! With this quality you Haripur girls will beat all women. What a hand for ladles !!
Sita: Ok ! Is it over…. Over now ?
Mandara: How can it be over. See the belching continues. *(Sita stood up to go)* Arre, getting up, no sit.

Sita:	Let me lift up the plates and clean up, I'll come certainly come and sit. See here I have tied seven knots at my saree edge. All matters will be discussed today.
Mandara:	What on earth (*Sita left. From outside Makunda's voice was heard*).
Makunda:	(*from outside*) Are you in the house, Sir !
Mandara:	Yes (*Immediately enters Makunda Swain, in a haughty mood. He is middle aged. Almost shaking in anger*).
Makunda:	You come outside Sir (to himself) arre ..... your day never ends unless five people insult you twenty five times... you will.....
Mandara:	What's the matter Makunda ?
Makunda:	You please come to the street, first .... Let the matter be discussed openly. Today, it's either his day or mine.
Mandara:	You 'll have your day outside, why should I go ?
Makunda:	Then, you decide my case.
Mandara:	Yes I'll ! You first settle down and sit.
Makunda:	How do you say to calm down, Sir ? Not once – not twice – he has cheated me ten times.
Radhu:	(*from outside*) Mohanty Sir, are you in the house ?
Makunda:	Look here, he's come. Following me he has come. You first come here !
Mandara:	Mukunda ! If you have come here respecting me as a guardian, listen to me and sit quite – Let him come here... Let the matter be open .....
Makunda:	Well then. People of the villages around listen

	to you, obey you – why shouldn't I obey – Yes I accept …. You decide my matter.
Radhu:	Mohanty Sir……….
Mandara:	Come here Radhu.
	(*Signalled at Makunda to sit quietly. Makunda sat quiet – Radhu pani entered*).
Mandara:	My brother- in- law….
Radhu:	What did you say ?
Mandara:	My brother-in-law has come from abroad to his village. He has sent for me Nainital potato and pure big halved Kanpuri dal. That dal was prepare at home with sweet and sour. O' what to say ! You will put aside the dal pot of Jagannath temple and eat that.
Radhu:	Do such things come in the fate of all ?
Mandara:	And what news Radhu – how are you here at this time ?
Radhu:	What for Makunda has come ?
Mandara:	I know why you have come – Makunda, speak the truth. How much Radhu owes your shop ?
Radhu:	Only five rupees. I was walking on the village road he shouts from behind, 'Hey Radhu Pani ! Give me my money !
Makunda:	It was my money. Yes I asked….
Radhu:	(*stopping him*) Shut up – why ask on the middle of the road. Do I not have any prestige ?
Makunda:	O' gosh, pres…ti…ge ! I asked for money therefore you abused me in filthy language – and now you attack me ? Come on, shell down my money.
Radhu:	I won't give you money.

Makunda:	You debtor....
Radhu:	Shut up....
Makunda:	Do you hear Sir ! You silly fool you'll not give my money ?
Radhu:	No – I won't give. I don't owe anything to your shop.... I don't know any money – foney –
Makunda:	Fine. Before Mohanty Sir the matter came and it is over – Ok you don't give me my money – yet Sir – listen to my words today – I too will not give.
Mandara:	Radhu says he won't pay your shop's debt money, what will you not give ?
Makunda:	Vote !
Mandara:	Vote ?
Makunda:	Yes vote. If five such customers come they will eat away my shop and wipe it clean. Could I be in this village that I'll give vote !
Radhu:	Hey you silly, is vote a donation for Dola – Dussera or matters of caste – if I sit to eat your leaf will be out !
Makunda:	If it's not caste matter, as agent why do you, one after another making Mahaprasad relations ? Why are you coaxing me last eight days to cast my vote in the Quill Pen box –
Mandara:	Listening to you I feel like laughing. Well, obey my words Radhu, return his money.
Radhu:	Let him agree to my views I'll give him his money.
Makunda:	Aha ! With my money you will buy my vote – How funny – do you see Sir.... What a dirty mind he has ....
Radhu:	Makunda....

Makunda:	I'll not give vote in the Quill Pen box – I'll give in my Minister's Umbrella box.
Mandara:	In about an hour there is a rally in the fair ground; you know that Makunda ?
Makunda:	I'm on my way to the rally.
Mandara:	The vote issue will be decided there; do you understand.
Makunda:	Unless the tangled issues of the village are solved the vote issue cannot be decided.
Mandara:	Alright, alright, that thing will be considered. Let today's rally be over. Hum Makunda, for your money I'm responsible – got it – now go.
	(Radhu and Makunda go out – Sita enters).
Sita:	Court is over ?
Mandara:	Dry court, dispersed on its own. Let your stubbornness relax first.
Sita:	Bijoy had come –
Mandara:	Which Bijoy ?
Sita:	Nuagam Sam Mohanty's son, Bijoy.
Mandara:	Why did he come here ?
Sita:	Why do you play oversmart ?.... Don't you know his uncle's house is in this village ?
Mandara:	O' I understand.
Sita:	Seba has fascinated him.
Mandara:	He too is not less attractive for Seba ?
Sita:	What about your mind ?
Mandara:	After elections –
Sita:	What ?
	(Sebati comes – a beautiful girl of 17/18. Comparatively modern although grown up in a village. She is wearing a plain saree).
Seba:	Bou, give me the almirah key.

Sita:	Why ?
Seba:	Oh' give ! (*taking the key she goes*).
Sita:	Seeing our daughter don't you feel ashamed ? How long will you keep her in the house ?
Mandara:	(*Rises*) In this No.11 Ward there are rich farmers – moneyed men also there – the educated are not less in number – but the perfect family boss (pointing at himself) only one !!
Sita:	O' What a capable man ! Every evening unless you run to the Jogi street for rice the pot will not go to the oven....
Mandara:	My capability is there only.... He who runs to the Jogi street to buy rice, why do people who have stocked bags of rice in their granary run to my house every morning ? Mandara Mohanty does not have an inch of land – but he has a handful of intelligence. What want ? In which thing there is want ? Haven't I constructed a brick – mortar house. No almirah, cot in the house – say – in which thing there is want ...... say, why don't you speak ?
	(*Sita could not control her laugh – she laughed in support of her husband, not derisively. Both laughed openly for a while – Seba came again. She is wearing a good saree and matching blouse – She is in a good mood*).
Seba:	Bou, bou –
Sita:	(*Looking at her with appreciating eyes*) Seba's aunt said the other day, if she wears her saree with folds who can say that she is a village girl ? (*Hearing bou's words Seba is pleased*)

Seba:	Take the key mother!
Sita:	Ok. You go and make two paans – I'm going.
Mandara:	Where?
Sita:	Since eight days, Brahmani auntie has sent word to go to her house. Today I plan to go but see, Seba is ready so early. (*Seba laughed*).
Seba:	Do you hear mother's words, father! As if I am ready to call on Brahmani auntie!
Sita:	Then, where will you go?
Seba:	Meeting!
Sita:	What?
Seba:	Don't you know today in the jatra grounds there is a meeting. Listen – what is written here…..
Sita:	What is that?
Seba:	Pamphlet – Bijoy bhai has given.
Sita:	What is there? What has Bijoy given?
Seba:	You listen, I'm reading (reads) 'A big rally in Nandipur Jatra grounds… the leader of United party (Quill Pen) and Ganasakti Dal (Umbrella) will speak to us about their views. After the rally there will be song dance'.
Mandara:	You support which Party dear?
Seba:	Bijoy Bhai's party.
Mandara:	What is that party?
Seba:	(*Showing a Quill Pen*) This party.
Mandara:	O' the United Party of Rajendra and Acharjya Babu – good, good good…
Sita:	Hey, she is going (*Seba goes out*) for some meeting and you say – gud, gud….
Mandara:	Such a big leader, Rajendra babu….. he is coming for the meeting with his wife. His wife is Chief Minister Mohapatra's daughter.

	Let Seba go with Bijoy, what's the harm ? And yes, have the knots in your saree edge loosened ?
Sita:	O' my burnt mind ? Look here – the younger daughter in law of the Sau family will sell a pair of pendants made of Jaypuri gold – will you keep ? Should I tell her ?
Mandara:	Yes I will – but after the vote…..
Sita:	What's this blasted vote vote you are talking about ? Tell me when the vote will be over ?
Mandara:	In one and half months. Let me go – I've to look at the organization of the rally.
Sita:	Listen – Sabitri ….
Mandara:	Who ?
Sita:	My younger sister Sabitri – she is nearing nine months. Should we not send gifts and things ?
Mandara:	Yes, after the votes.
Sita:	O' listen to him ! everything after the votes….
Mandara:	Look here – he who is a farmer he gives word give and take – after November, the harvesting season – The businessman says, after the debts are recovered, the service holder says after the Ist of the month. At present call it my 1st of the month or November full moon day everything is vote – do you get it ? I am going – don't you call me from behind……
Sita:	Break my head, but listen to one more thing –
Mandara:	What other knot remained ?
Sita:	The same vote thing –
Mandara:	Hain ! You and vote ??

Sita:	O' he ! My maternal uncle's son's father-in-law's nephew's nephew…
Mandara:	Wait ! Wait ! Your maternal uncle's son's that thing… that thing… will be what to me ?
Sita:	How funny ! If he is my distant cousin brother what's he to you….
Mandara:	Ok…. He is your brother… is that not enough !
Sita:	He is contesting in the elections…… what Mahapatra who is a Minister ?
Mandara:	I understand !!! What do you say ?
Sita:	What is his box ?
Mandara:	Umbrella box –
Sita:	My auntie has requested me like anything in her message – to cast my vote in the Umbrella box, - see that box wins.
Mandara:	Father – mother and daughter we are three persons in this house. Daughter's Quill Pen box, yours' Umbrella box –
Sita:	And yours ?
Mandara:	Mine ! On two sides of my shirt are two open boxes. As you two's boxes will fill up my pocket boxes too will fill up with notes. After the elections – you understand now ? I am going.

■

Act I : Scene – vi

(The Jatra grounds of Nandipur. The rally is over. At the meeting place are only two, Makunda and Radhu Pani. When the curtain goes up it is seen that Radhu has forcibly pressed down the hands of Makunda.)

Makunda:	No, no, no – that thing never. I've one father – one word – I won't cast my vote in the Quill Pen box.
Radhu:	Why not ?
Makunda:	I won't give – What's this, why ?
Radhu:	You have to give.
Makunda:	I won't give come what may.
Radhu:	Makunda ! Listen to me I say otherwise I won't allow you to live in this village.
Makunda:	O' save me ! – before elections he is already a Minister –
Radhu:	Hey Makunda ! Such a big rally was held, you heard from so many big shots so many things and in the end you say….
Makunda:	None said whether Sita was female or male. Well, tell me. What kind of rally was this ? This side's secret follies they opened up and asked us to vote for Quill Pen. They sang their – own praise and said vote in the Umbrella box, and our Mohanty babu who was President, he said in such a manner that, 'the snake will not die, the stick will not

	break'. From this what will you understand – Sita male or female ?
Radhu:	What more could they have spoken ? We heard the two sides – now you think and consider and vote as you think proper.
Makunda:	Yes that's good. I'll do what my conscience will decide. Whey then do you try to motivate me ?
Radhu:	Hey, you can't be counted as a man – these are matters of high politics – I am explaining to you because you can't understand.
Makunda:	Haa ! Since becoming an agent, like the well dressed cheats you are wearing clean clothes. Has the waist tightened ?
Radhu:	What do you mean, I eat money. You stupid, do I earn money in corrupt ways ?
Makunda:	If you don't take money, how do you say to pay me back my money tomorrow ? Where from will you get money ?
Radhu:	You, fellow, are inhuman, the baggage porter of idiots. If there are no agents, how can there be elections ? Raghu Patnaik is an agent of the Umbrella party – does he then make money ?
Makunda:	Yes he does, from my shop he has taken one kg of cow ghee. He was not getting even dry wicks – today as the babus came, his value rises. He is as you are. There – Babu has come (*Mandara Mohanty comes*) Sir – please explain to us.
Mandara:	What ?
Makunda:	This…….
Radhu:	(*Cutting him*) Wait you fool – listen. (*To Mandara*) gave a fine lecture, is it not Sir ?

Mandara: Who?
Radhu: Acharjya. The Jute episode has been appreciated by the other side. Didn't you see how they burst out clapping?
Makunda: Umbrella too came up well. What's his name – yes, Sharma. The way he hit, there were waves of applause – no Sir?
Mandara: Both were right. This side said so much Jute is produced in our state, goes to Bengal – the middlemen take all the profit, yet our Government do not set up Jute Mills here – the United Party shouts against that. But the day Govt. set up Jute Mills, the next day these people will gather and brainwashing the workers will organize strikes, and plan to remove the Mill –
Radhu: Is this right?
Mandara: I don't say this is right, Radhu. I say this is right and that is also right.
Makunda: Yes, they are as these are.
Mandara: I'm an impartial man. Both are equal in my eyes. The meeting ended. I took the Quill Pen people to their camp and the Umbrella people to their bunglow. Well – let me go and have a round Makunda! What have you decided? Who would you vote?
Makunda: In the Umbrella box – you say both are equal – when I have made friendship with the Umbrella people for five years, why break it now?
Radhu: Do shameless people grow on trees? Sala has made friendship! In the last five years they have looted and cleaned up. You will vote for them again?

Makunda:	Sir, all these people say Govt. was corrupt and looted money – what did they loot ? Is it a foreign Govt. so that he will go home taking on his head: our brother ate away our things, let him eat – how much will he eat……
Radhu:	(Shouting) Ma – ku – nda –
Makunda:	What you'll hit me ?
Mandara:	Just listen to him Radhu, what he speaks. Yes what were you speaking Makunda ?
Makunda:	I say if Govt. loots money, when Quill Pen comes won't they do the same ? Do they not have needs and desires ?
Radhu:	You know Makunda. I will break your head.
Makunda:	O' gosh what a hero ! If my words hurt why do you coax me like this for a vote ? I say Sir, ours is the same Umbrella box. Their pot is now full like the ghee – absorbing pot, there is already a layer of cream. Those who will form the new Government, they must set up a new pot, another five years. Like this one, after five years another pot will have layers of cream and our pot will turn turtle –
Radhu:	Do you hear Sir, This idiot's words –
Mandara:	Yes I'm listening his words and also yours – I am neutral, for me you are right and he is also right (*goes out*).
Makunda:	Do you understand, Umbrella is as Quill Pen.
Radhu:	(*Softly*) Hey Maku…..
Makunda:	O' stop your flattering ! Maku will no more fall into your trap…. See here, the Kataki babu is coming. –

(*Enters Sashi. An educated city youth, a bag and camera in his hand*).

Radhu:	Come Sir ! You haven't gone to the camp ?
Sashi:	Heard, some song and dance programme is there. Where is Bijoy Babu ?
Radhu:	He has gone to make arrangements.
Makunda:	Our village Jatra party will present a farcical play.
Sashi:	How late will that be ? (*As if searching for some one*).
Makunda:	No, it will begin now. Don't you see, how men and women are coming in groups to see the play – Are you from Cuttack ?
Sashi:	Yes.
Makunda:	Are you serving in the vote area –
Radhu:	He is an idiot Sir, don't listen to him.
Makunda:	I ask because, I don't know ..... why shouldn't he listen to me ?
Sashi:	No, I'm not serving.
Makunda:	Sir –
Radhu:	This gentleman is the private secretary to Acharjya Sir.
Makunda:	Whatever – it's some kind of job .... Must be getting a salary .... Otherwise.
Sashi:	No, no. I'm not serving nor am I taking salary. After completing my education I'm with Acharjya Sir. I'm helping him in the election work –
Makunda:	Like that ..... eating from your pocket !!
Sashi:	You know what a great man he is !! If one lives with him one learns many things.
Makunda:	O' you ... what's it called ..... learning ! Training ! After which you will be appointed.
Sashi:	That girl ?
Radhu:	Who ?

Sashi:	That one who during the meeting....
Makunda:	O' Sebati –
Sashi:	Yes, Sebati.
Makunda:	There, she is standing in that group of women. Shall I call her ? (*Called out*) SEBATI – he...
Radhu:	Makunda –
Makunda:	What, shall I not call her....
Sashi:	No, let it be – (*goes away, Radhu followed his path meaningfully.... Makunda at first could not understand any thing. Later by following the route Radhu Pani's eyes surveyed, he could understand every thing*).
Makunda:	O' gosh ! Radhu Pani ! This mischief is going on ! Arre hey ! The other's pen can never be yours. She, after all is Mandara Mohanty's daughter, she will weave such a plot that even a Prince will go playing the lyre as a Yogi –

{ S O N G }

(*After the entertainment programme starts, enter Acharjya, Rajendra, Gita and their co-workers from the United party. From the ruling party enter Sharma and his colleagues. With them also came Mandara Mohanty, Sebati, Bijoy and others – Acharjya and Sharma sat in the chairs marked for them. The President Mandara Mohanty took his seat. Sebati stood near Gita. Through dance and music the Ganasakti Party was sharply attacked. The dance ended. The dance party left – Acharjya, Sharma and others stood up*).

Makunda:	(*Respectfully*) These four are our village Jatra Party boys.
Radhu:	(*Without being heard by others*) Makunda...
Makunda:	(*To Radhu*) why, am I speaking rot (*to others*) In the old days did they not have such farces

	like Gayasura Badha, Sudharma Sabha – they practiced many such farces. This time they have learnt many social farces from the cinema at Cuttack.
Sharma:	Yes, they have imitated them well (*to Mandara*) Now give us leave….
Makunda:	(*folding his hands*) I have one thing to say before you great people.
Radhu:	Makunda –
Makunda:	I'm not educated, I ask because I don't know.
Sharma:	Ok, speak what you wish to.
Makunda:	Sir ! The meeting was held. We heard both sides… we'll all give votes – your highness will form Government. We'll live in peace, but who has sent you to form government ? (*None understood anything else more than Makunda's idiocy*)
Sharma:	Why should anyone send ? We have come here on our own.
Makunda:	Exactly that thing Sir ! – For our comfort and convenience you people enduring all heat and dust, run to our doors spending money from your pockets. Thirst goes to water, but how does water go to the thirsty ? I couldn't understand this complex thing.
Radhu:	Do you understand now ?
Makunda:	As if you have understood every thing !
Sharma:	No has he understood anything Makunda, why water comes to thirst – raising this matter you have shaken democracy to its foundations. Whoever gives answer to your question, vote for him.
Sashi:	You cannot answer this question ?

Sharma: No, let him answer who can (*to Mandara*) well, now give us leave.

Mandara: (In a hurry) what a man am I Sir - What leave can I give you Sir !

(After exchanging salutations Sharma and his friends take leave, Mandara went along with them)

Makunda: (*Alone to Sashi*) Did I do anything wrong Sir!

Rajendra: No, you haven't done anything wrong. Now tell me first, what government is going on in our state.

Makunda: (*Thinking for a while*) Umbrella government. (*All laugh*)

Rajendra: I'm not asking about that. Foreign rule, royalty are now gone – now –

Makunda: Sir, Minister Rule –

Rajendra: Ok – but like the king's son becoming king minister's son can not be minister. Where from will ministers come ? Some one from among us will become minister.

Makunda: Yes they become ! Our Seb Bou's uncle's father-in-law's son's relation has become minister.

Rajendra: But how could he become minister ?

Makunda: That thing hajoor I don't understand. I fall sick, I should go to the doctor's door or the doctors' smelling the disease come to my door ?

Acharjya: You can't understand this so easily Makunda. Wait. Gradually you'll understand. You simply know this much that to form a strong government in our state we must vote for the right persons. Do you get it ?

Makunda: Got it Sir, yet hearing two versions from two

	sides at times I am confused….
Radhu:	Makunda !! (*wielding authority*)
Makunda:	O' gosh, Sir ! Radhu Pani won't allow me here anymore – let me go. (*bends and salutes goes out followed by Radhu Pani*)
Sashi:	This song and dance programme perhaps hurt Mr. Sharma – he went away without saying anything on that.
Acharjya:	What's there to hurt ? The true picture of the state is given there. Who had organized these programmes ?
Sashi:	Bijoya babu and this girl ?
Acharjya:	O' he has ! – who is this girl ?
Sashi:	Tell him Bijoya Babu –
Bijaya:	She is Sebati – he who presided today –
Acharjya:	O' Sri Mandara Mohanty's daughter !
Bijaya:	Yes.
Gita:	Do you always stay in the village ?
Sebati:	Yes.
Gita:	In this election will you help us….
Sashi:	They are already doing – day and night they are working for our party.
Acharjya:	Really ?
Sashi:	An enthusiastic worker like him is not found in this area.
Acharjya:	Glad to hear that Sebati ! We don't have the affluence to give you a gold chain, this is your prize (*gives a garland to Sebati*).
Sashi:	(*claps*) Your good luck Sebati, tomorrow this news will be flashed in the papers – In this age, a great peoples hero Sri Ramnarayana Acharjya, - how he felicitates a simple village girl.

Bijaya:	On the election day how all the village women can come and vote – that responsibility has been taken by Sebati.
Rajendra:	In which box you will cast your vote ?
Sebati:	Quill Pen box – only excepting my mother.
Gita:	Why ? Why should your mother be excepted?
Sebati:	Chief Minister is her maternal cousin's father-in-law's cousin brother's nephew, therefore her vote will go into the Umbrella box.
Rajendra:	And you ! Why should you vote for us ?
Sebati:	Because due to the incompetence of this government the state is going to hell. In this situation only the United Party alone can save the state.
Gita:	Who has given you this lesson, Sebati ?
Sashi:	From Bijoy Babu – he is her teacher.
Rajendra:	(*Placing both his hands on the shoulders of Bijoy*) You can Bijoy. You have the ability to know the state. But 'playing with fire' – that matter you shouldn't forget.
Acharjya:	Where is your father gone, Sebati – here he comes (*Mandara enters*).
Mandara:	Excuse me Sir ! I went to see them off.
Acharjya:	Now, give us leave.
Mandara:	What insignificant man I am Sir ! What farewell can I give you ?
Rajendra:	You are a neutral person, you say – what will be the result of this election ?
Mandara:	In this election, I have locked up my mouth, don't you see – all the people of this village are madly involved – yet my mouth is closed.

Acharjya:	But if you don't open your mouth, at the right time all mouths will be shut. You may not know – the villagers will cast their vote – somehow or other I can't believe it.
Mandara:	No Sir ! What a man am I ?
Acharjya:	(*Knitting his brows looks intently at Mandara*) Well, come let's go. We have to cover twenty more miles today. (*Mandara led the way with alacrity. The others followed but almost immediately Sebati returned – she had hung the flower garland on a chair, given by Acharjya – While taking it she noticed a bag kept on the chair, while picking it up and turning, Sashi came*).
Sashi:	You won't forget us Sebati ?
Sebati:	For you people, I can even sacrifice my life.
Sashi:	Like Bijoy babu you too can Sebati – You have not only patriotism, (*swallowing saliva*) You have life, you have heart. – That bag that's not Bijoy babu's – its mine.
Sebati:	(*Giving the bag she was about to leave*) Please stand for a while, Sebati ! I will take a picture of you.
Sebati:	Why ?
Sashi:	I said, you have life, you have heart, just stand a bit, (*Sebati stood as if she was in an awkward situation*) I don't know who got what in the Nandipur rally but what I got….. yes, smile please – if you don't laugh how can you make those people laugh for whom you have tightened your belt ? Laugh ! (*Sebati laughed, Sashi clicked a photo*).

■

Act - II: Scene – i

(A room in the house of Mandara Mohanty. The room is decorated according to his status – A cot with proper mattress – Sita is asleep on her side. At the front of the stage Mandara is standing. He is twirling his moustache with his right hand. The left hand is resting on a cane stick. A sign of victory in his face)

Mandara: Flattened ……. *(Sita looked angrily at him)* flattened. *(Sita in anger turned to the other side)*…. Flattened !

Sita: I'll commit suicide. I say – kill myself.

Mandara: Aha ! ha ha – Seba bou – have some patience. Your maternal cousin's father-in-law's …..

Sita: Again you are teasing me ? I'll jump into a well or pond…. Shall eat poison. You being my own person you don't give me peace for a moment. How can I walk among my friends and foes ? At home and outside, all of you have taken your revenge on me. Born from my own womb even Seba is not mine. That Radhu Pani, can he be counted as a man – He will tell me…..

Mandara: Flattened ! …. O' this much ? *(This time Sita cried bitterly and struck her head on the wall)* Oh ! O' my Seba's mother – listen to me – please hear me –

Sita:	What to hear – this blasted election – only my luck turned turtle. I have no place among my own people –
Mandara:	Hey Seba's mother ! In this vote six to seven hundred people lost. Mortgaging land, selling ornaments they fought election spending thousands. Three hundred lost their deposits. They have started living normal life – You went running to put your vote in the Umbrella box for your maternal cousin's sake. And simply for this your brothers and friends are cut off from you ? Fie, fie he who hears this…..
Sita:	Don't say so much ! People living in the world, what not do they do ? When wife opens her mouth husband builds a bridge to Lanka. I never asked for money or jewellery, made a fervent request to see that the umbrella box wins the vote. Did you keep my words ? And over that you say –
Mandara:	Flattened !! Listen, Seba's mother. I'm a neutral person.
Sita:	To hell with your side. If you are neutral where is that Quill Pen ?
Mandara:	None knew so long, I'm telling you today, look here, - my ballot paper is as such in my pocket. I haven't given my vote to anyone. If the Umbrella box would have won – this Mohapatra would have written 'Mohanty you are a solid man: Quill Pen has won. Mr. Acharjya has written – Mohanty, our Party won, we'll rule over the state. But we remain indebted to you. Do you understand ?

Sita:	You know only that – before the king son and before the queen, daughter.
Mandara:	Aha ! If the king and the queen are happy what's wrong in making the son, daughter and the daughter, son ? Why should that pain me ?
Sita:	What will I get from all that ? My words were not kept.
Mandara:	Which matter was not kept – the ear rings of the younger daughter-in-law of the Sahu house.
Sita:	Is that there ? Go see Radhu Pani's wife's ears.
Mandara:	Your sister's pregnancy gift –
Sita:	That would have waited for you !
Mandara:	Arre whether it has gone or not ?
Sita:	Aha ha ha –
Mandara:	Then it has gone. What remains then ? Yes Seba's marriage. That will be done in such splendour and pomp....
Sita:	What will happen.... Have you seen almanac ? In the new almanac there is no marriage for thirteen months.
Makunda:	*(From outside)* Mohanty Sir ! Are you there ?
Mandara:	Yes.
Makunda:	Where ?
Mandara:	Come to this room *(Sita goes. Makunda enters).*
Makunda:	What is this tamsa going on Sir !
Mandara:	Tamasa !
Makunda:	Whatever was to happen has happened – Whoever wanted to loot, looted by force. Now they must live normally or should they split hairs –

Mandara:	Understood – Where's the other ?
Makunda:	Why should I know where he went ?
Radhu:	*(Outside)* Mohanty Sir, are you there ?
Mandara:	Yes, yes (*To Makunda)* See, here he comes.
Makunda:	Let him come *(Radhu enters)*.
Radhu:	What ! *(To Makunda)* Umbrella holding emperor Sri Sri Sri Makunda Deb ! Your silk – Umbrella flattened ?
Makunda:	So what ?
Radhu:	What so what ?
Makunda:	You've opened the Purana – Ok sing as much you wish –
Radhu:	Are you angry Maku ! I went to your house and came searching for you. It seems during election you have snatched three brand new Umbrellas, give me one – Ok, I'll pay you, I don't ask for free.
Makunda:	Listen to him, Sir !
Radhu:	No, not lies – yesterday in the whirlwind my Umbrella turned and was flattened. Gone totally, the handle and all broken to pieces. Without Umbrella how can I manage ? Give me one.
Makunda:	I say this having you as witness, Sir – hereafter don't blame me – what if your wooden handle is broken in pieces – the day Makunda Soin rises your hands and legs will be broken to smithereens – you know ? Have I flown into this village from somewhere else ?
Radhu:	Don't utter the village name – I won't allow you to live in this village – the roads, ghats, the air, water is forbidden for you. This year

	I'll show you the five pilgrimages – you think I'm the same Radhu Pani ! This morning when the Daroga saw me, immediately he got off from the cycle and said – O' Radhu Babu !
Makunda:	O' what a hero !
Radhu:	It's there, yes noted already. Makunda Soin has cast this number vote in the Umbrella box. You know, in a month there will be eleven cases against you. I won't allow you even a straw in your thatched roof.
Makunda:	For how many days ? For how long this temper ? Lord Ram went to the forest for fourteen years – did Ajodhya remain or was swept away ? Five years will pass in a trice – then ? *(Mandara Mohanty was happily making paan)*.
Mandara:	Hey Makunda, Radhu is just teasing you, why do you take it so seriously ?
Makunda:	What is he to me Sir, to tease me ?
Mandara:	You have done wrong Makunda !
Makunda:	Stab me at the throat Sir ! If you say this simply because I cast my vote in the Umbrella box –
Mandara:	Arre no Umbrella or handle – this is election – confidential. The vote box is in a secret place. Whether you have given to the snake or frog, Indra and Moon did not know. How convenient ?
Makunda:	He says he has noted the number.
Mandara:	Joke ! See me, I am neutral, yet. When Quill party won – out of 140 in the Assembly occupied 101 seats – Quietly turn to them.

	Who can save you if you turn against the Government ?
Makunda:	How am I involved Sir, why should I be a rebel to Government.
Mandara:	Oho ! You don't get it. If they come to know that such and such man from such and such village is raising hulla – then ? Who loses ?
Makunda:	Ok Sir ! I'll keep your word . I'am at your mercy – do as you please.
Mandara:	You go there – no one can do anything to you, I'am there – go…
Radhu:	Hey Makunda – today there will be a dance, do you know ! Your charge is to arrange leaf and water for them – if you don't do it –
Makunda:	O' I'm so afraid… *(goes. Mandara laughs)*
Mandara:	He's a simpleton ! Yes. Radhu what news ?
Radhu:	The same thing Sir –
Mandara:	What thing ?
Radhu:	That….
Mandara:	That, what ?
Radhu:	The villagers are agitated –
Mandara:	Tell them – The day I die let them not prepare my *Kokei' (Kokei is a carrier made of bamboo for the dead body)* – Am I Makunda Soin ?
Radhu:	They make my life miserable – I had given word to them on your behalf …..
Mandara:	Did I say eat from the Umbrella party and insert in the Quill Pen box ?
Radhu:	Umbrella became cautions – gave nothing –
Mandara:	And Quill Pen has poured ! Shameless !!
Radhu:	You please come.
Mandara:	Ok let's go. You understand Radhu, where Mandara Mohanty gets involved there he

	sacrifices everything – but when there is any real issues, there nothing – no movement. O' Seba ! Seba *(Seba comes)* Where's your mother gone ?
Seba:	To call on brahmani auntie.
Mandara:	Ok. Come Radhu *(both go out)* *(Sebati lifted out an almanac and turned its pages. After a while Mandara returned and Sebati went inside).*
Mandara:	Come Babu, come inside *(Sashi followed).* This morning after getting up I definitely saw auspicious signs – your feet fell in my house. Please sit.
Sashi:	For me you will be delayed for your work
Mandara:	What work ?
Sashi:	You were going out somewhere...
Mandara:	O' that thing ! Without me these villagers will not do anything – but you first or the villagers first ? How heartening that you people have won – Acharjya became Chief Minister..... Who are the other ministers ?
Sashi:	Rajendra Babu, Debanand Babu but .... Let go, that discussion all the time is getting on the nerves. Now tell me about you, everything is fine ?
Mandara:	Perhaps you know, I don't own an inch of land. Yet you will see me like this everyday.
Sashi:	How is Sebati ?
Mandara:	Why do you ask ! Not that the United Party won – but she as if has the golden moon in her hand.
Sashi:	Is she not at home ?
Mandara:	Yes she was – take a paan *(opening the box)*

	gosh – there is no paan – Hey Seba – see here, who has come…. She is very bashful – here she comes *(Sebati came and silently saluted him)*
Sashi:	Namaskar! How are you?
Sebati:	Fine, haven't you met Bijoy Bhai?
Sashi:	*(As if afraid)* Where is he?
Mandara:	Bijoy had come?
Sebati:	Yes, I sent for him *(Sashi is dissatisfied hearing about Bijoy)*
Sashi:	No, Ok – I've no time to sit – I'll go to Cuttack by this 2.0'clock train.
Sebati:	Please convey my Namaskara to Gita Devi.
Sashi:	Alright.
Mandara:	*(Indicating)* Give him paan.
Sashi:	No paan I don't want. *(But his hand automatically stretched while Sebati was giving paan to Mandara).*
Sashi:	O' I had forgotten …. here *(takes out a gold chain from his pocket and gives it to Mandara)*
Mandara:	For whom is this chain?
Sashi:	This is the prize for Sebati for her good work during the election.
Mandara:	Who has given?
Sashi:	What will you get from that? You know, I'm Mr. Acharjya's man – I was given the responsibility of giving a gold chain to Sebati – that I have fulfilled. Well! Sir! I'm coming. Namaskara *(goes out)*
	(from inside comes Sita. Who has heard everything)
Sita:	Who is he?
Mandara:	He is…..

Sita:	Why has he given a gold chain to my daughter ?
Mandara:	O' returning from your street town. You were listening everything ?
Sita:	Aren't you ashamed ? You speak shaking your head – telling you in earnest, return that chain to him.
Mandara:	He must have fled on his cycle. Where will I look for him now ?
Sita:	Who told you to keep it ? Is he such a giver ? He'll give a gold chain to my daughter ! I would have torn him apart and eaten away his lever.
Mandara:	Why didn't you ? Why did you hide yourself under a seven yard veil ? Ok he has given so it's given. When I go to Cuttack, I will ask Acharjya – who has given the necklace – if he has given then it's fine…. Here … keep it.
Sita:	I' won't touch it. You have kept, you know what to do – Arre ! What did he think of my daughter ? I was opposed to it, but you made my daughter dance in the election. Now enjoy the results. That necklace will not enter my house – you take it , dig a hole and keep it wherever you please.
Mandara:	What are you talking about ? What have I got ? You are surpassing your limits.
Sita:	What face have you kept of me that I will surpass. Embracing other men you have painted your own people with six layers of lime and ink….
Mandara:	Arre…. The person is now possessed by witches. That one thing she is repeating. This

Sita:	woman is out to break the house. You know that make and break art – those things are not in my horoscope.
Mandara:	Hey Seba's mother…. Keep this necklace I say –
Sita:	Don't tell me about the chain – don't tell me – the wanton rises in me….
Mandara:	*(Angrily)* If your maternal uncle's this thing and that thing had given this necklace – this you would have burst out crying ! What else should I speak… Ok go go !

Act - I I: Scene – ii

(A city road. From one side comes Bijoy and from the other, Sashi)

Sashi: Oho ! Bijoy Babu, namaskara, namaskara – seeing you after many days. Since that Nandipur rally day I haven't seen you. When did you come to Cuttack ?
Bijoy: I'm always here.
Sashi: Always means ?
Bijoy: It's now three months. I came here the day the Ministry was formed. Haven't returned.
Sashi: Where do you stay ?
Bijoy: In the Party office. You never go that side...
Sashi: No time.. Mr. Acharjya became Chief Minister – Secretary – Private Secretary, in all six salaried servants but he won't leave me alone...
Bijoy: How many have this kind of luck ?
Sashi: *(Looking at a different thing)* See Bijoy Babu, is he not Sharma ? Yes, Sharma where's he heading that way ?
Bijoy: This time he has not been eliminated ?
Sashi: No, poor chap, just escaped. The bloke had thought this country is his maternal property. Will be on the seat of power all the time. He got the taste this time ! Do you think because of mal administration of government, he was unpopular and was

	defeated ? No – the reason why Ganasakti Party lost is – internal power struggle ! Ok Bijoy Babu, let me go. You have seen my house. Come this evening – I'm not sticking to Mr. Acharjaya for a long time.
Bijoy:	Why ?
Sashi:	How much can I work and for what ? A Calcutta businessman has started a new project here. I'll manage his business. There's power and also comfort. There must be a beautiful house like a picture – in the evening hours I'll be listening to music on radio cylone. An expensive car for tours – fat pay packet ! To tell you the truth somehow or other my mind is now anxious to enjoy life.
Bijoy:	I have some misgivings Sashi Babu, winning the election these people have formed the government – if they can't fulfill promises ! It's only three months but the news papers have started writing against them.
Sashi:	That's nonsense. If you do politics you must have patience for criticism. Does that mean that they will run the government being afraid of people ?
Bijoy:	The rural voters are now impatient – when good days would come to them ?
Sashi:	What, within three months ?
Bijoy:	Yes, today only I got a letter from Sebati.
Sashi:	Sebati.... Sebati *(pretending not to know)* O' that Sebati of yours – how is she ?
Bijoy:	Fine.
Sashi:	I'm coming. Namaskar. *(goes)*.

■

Act - I I: Scene – iii

(A room in the official accommodation of Minister Rajendra – private – decorated in simple style. When the scene begins it is seen that Rajendra Babu is in an easy chair. A long letter in his hand – the letter has not pleased him, that impression comes out of his appearance. Moreover he is at present ill. He has not broken down but he is apparently sick. He folds the letter and places it on the table nearby and rings the calling bell – enters Gita holding a glass of fruit juice)

Gita:	Here, take it. *(Rajendra never expected that Gita would come responding to the bell)*
Rajendra:	You ?
Gita:	Take this –
Rajendra:	Sherbet ?
Gita:	*(Proffered her hand)* yes.
Rajendra:	*(Holding it)* What sherbet is this ?
Gita:	Fruit juice.
Rajendra:	Fruit...
Gita:	Yes, grapes, pine apple, pomegranate and lemon....
Rajendra:	Gita.... !! *(Gita looked hurt)* Don't you know Gita while I'm drinking fruit juice millions of my people.
Gita:	*(emotionally)* I know, I know – while you are drinking fruit juice here millions of your countrymen do not get even a cup of rice

	gruel. But for that why should I suffer this punishment ? Your physical condition today -
Rajendra:	How many people have the condition to think about their body ?
Gita:	But why do you forget that the salary which you get from the tax money of the countrymen, I don't spend a pie out of it towards this. I know the responsibility of saving the country today has been given to you: but the countrymen have not taken the responsibility of saving you nor can they ever take. That responsibility is mine, mine alone ! Don't prevent me from that.
Rajendra:	I understand what you mean Gita ! But I don't understand why I become so very helpless ?
Gita:	The doctor has said you should not try to understand anything. And you have given word you will not protest against my work for the next six months –
Rajendra:	Let it be so Gita. Let the six months go like child's play. Today I drink this costly fruit juice. No one will open his mouth to say that this is not right; but that silence will one day demand explanation from me. Ministership is not the exercise of power – nor is it a job – ministership is service and sacrifice I want to live only for these values *(drinks the juice) – he rings the calling bell, but none came)*
Gita:	Who do you want ?
Rajendra:	Orderly. P.A. ?
Gita:	They are not here –

Rajendra: None have come?
Gita: None.
Rajendra: Why?
Gita: Seeing your condition they too took pity on you. They don't want you to work for now.
Rajendra: No file has come today?
Gita: No –
Rajendra: Then I'll go to the Secretariat myself. I'll take today's salary or not?
Gita: No, from today begins your leave.
Rajendra: From today? Who said? I haven't got any reply from Mr. Acharjya.
Gita: I requested him personally – you will go on leave for six months from today – he has agreed.
Rajendra: Agreed!! You say correctly Gita, - he has agreed?
Gita: Yes.
Rajendra: (Thinking for a while) I get it, but – how will I spend this long six months? When I look back the past ten years, even ten days I haven't spent in laziness. And long six months! I'm afraid Gita – on whose support these long vacant days I'll spend? – Who?
(*He didn't get any scope to speak further, Gita was standing behind his chair. Suddenly she sang just a snatch of a song near Rajendra's ears. For some time Rajendra's eyes closed*)
Rajendra: Only a woman can discover the lively feelings hidden in the dry and juiceless interior of a man's heart! You cannot be avoided Gita!
Gita: Such transformatory qualities in just a snatch of a song!

Rajendra:	Not the effect of the song but the effect of Gita !
Gita:	*(Picking up the Bhagabata Gita from the table)* The effect of this Gita !
Rajendra:	This Bhagabata Gita – here Lord Krishna proving all of life's unrealities to Arjun inspires him to be a very complex worldly man ! This is a Oxymoron to achieve your goals. You are following the same path ?
Gita:	It's not right for you to strain your mind over anything whereas you have started convincing me –
Rajendra:	Somebody came perhaps *(Gita went to the door)*
Gita:	*(Greets with Namaskara)* Uncle ! You suddenly ? *(Sharma enters. Rajendra salutes him)*
Rajendra:	Please sit down !
Sharma:	*(To Gita)* You were saying something – I barged in suddenly – but it is not correct to say that I came suddenly. After five months of your marriage, this is the first time I have come.
Rajendra:	But why should you hesitate to come here ?
Sharma:	You and Gita got married. Then came the election – in the election your party won – we lost – you became Minister. If you add up these things I feel there is a wall between us.
Rajendra:	It's good you came. Please say what we have done or not done during the first three months of our government – what do you think ?

Sharma:	Excuse me Rajendra Babu – what you have done or not done it's account we'll give in the next session of the Assembly. I have not come for that discussion. Tell me how are you.
Rajendra:	I am not well, but...
Sharma:	No if and buts you must take complete rest.
Rajendra:	Yes, taking........ Cigarette ?
Sharma:	Sorry I won't take. I heard you have given up cigarettes ?
Rajendra:	Yes.
Sharma:	What, for your bad health ?
Rajendra:	No, not for that.
Sharma:	No I remember ! You gave up cigarettes after becoming minister – it came out in the papers.
Rajendra:	How such small things go to newspapers !
Sharma:	A minister giving up cigarette is not a small thing ! Moreover it is sensational news for the hawkers' call.
Rajendra:	I haven't given up smoking with any motive or to preach an ideal.
Sharma:	Perhaps you don't know why you have given up cigarettes, but in the tea shops and river side benches this must have been discussed by many and views in your favour and negative comments must have come from many mouths. *(Somebody perhaps came from outside – Rajendra himself went to the door – Gita came from inside a cup of tea in hand).*
Gita:	*(to Sharma)* Please take.
	(She proferred the cup to Sharma – at the

selfsame time Rajendra ushered in Chief Minister Mr. Acharjya – his demeanor shows that he is not the old Acharjya. Not that his pride or arrogance has increased as he is now the CM; but there is apparent a superiority complex which he wears naturally and he likes to show that. His demeanor also suggests that he does not want to waste a minute anywhere. Besides this all the signs of an experienced leader are reflected in his face. As he entered his eyes fell on Sharma, and also the scene of the tea cup offered by Gita and taken by him. He has assessed the situation. But that he was the CM of the state and deserved all attention was evident in his bearing. But the same diplomatic smile in his face...Sharma never expected to meet Acharjya there. Then he debated silently whether he should stay or leave. He kept the cup on a table. Gita in silence paid her respects to Acharjya)

Sharma: Namaskar *(Gita went inside)*

Acharjya: *(Smiling)* What's the news Mr. Abadhut ? How far your anniversary celebration has gone ? We often discuss your matters – is it not Rajendra Babu !

Sharma: Do you remember Nandipur Rally ?

Acharjya: Who will ever forget that ? In an election rally two opposing parties speaking together is a rare sight in our country.

Sharma: That day I had celebrated my anniversary – after the meeting the dance and music was meant for my adulation – I have taken it like that.

(Acharjya burst out laughing choicelessly – he was saved by Gita who handed him over a glass of juice)-

Gita: Vimto.....

Acharjya: *(taking the glass)* Vimto ! O' my favorite drink. Thank you *(drinks)* You know Mr. Sharma – we have decided, this time we will give 30 percent of seats to women. *(Gita went inside).*

Sharma: On this I totally agree with you; but not women only – both wife and husband must be given chance to become Assembly members.

Acharjya: Why ?

Sharma: For birth control or planned parenthood – in the Assembly debates the scope for table thumping by men and women members will be almost eliminated.

Acharjya: *(Smiling)* You must then be given this chance first.

Sharma: Ok by me. But my wife will never agree to be a member of the Assembly. Because she has been functioning as speaker of the forty member home Assembly of our five brother families. She has no desire to be just a member.

(This time also Acharjya laughed like the previous time. Gita came with a plate for Acharjya).

Gita: Areca nuts and masala.

Acharjya: Thanks.

Sharma: Let me now take leave –

Gita: Your tea !....

Acharjya: Yes, you haven't taken your tea.

Sharma:	It's cold.
Gita:	Please wait, let me bring hot tea.
Sharma:	You brought hot tea – I couldn't drink it and made it cold *(looking sharply at Acharjya)*. The tea is not to blame – the fault is mine. Therefore its not meet that I should take tea. I'm coming…. Namaskar …..*(Goes out)*
Acharjya:	How is your health Rajendra Babu ?
Rajendra:	Not at all good.
Acharjya:	You should take rest very soon. I have arranged for the sanction of your leave from today…. Where do you propose to go ?
Gita:	Switzerland …
Acharjya:	I was exactly thinking like that – you should stay in Switzerland for a few days – And yes, whatever you spend will be reimbursed by government.
Rajendra:	No !
Acharjya:	No !!
Rajendra:	Money has been arranged.
Acharjya:	How come ? I know you do not have any resource.
Rajendra:	Gita has sold all her property and the money is kept in the bank. My medical expenses are met from that money.
Acharjya:	Alright. Hum, the proposal you sent to government that after your expenses, the rest of your salary you will return to government – do you believe that's right ? What do you say ? Ok, you first come back after your leave. Don't you worry Gita Devi – my blessings and by the good wishes of the people Rajendra Babu will return hale and hearty very soon.

(Gita just smiled and went in with cups and glasses)

Rajendra: Read this letter.

Acharjya: Letter ! Who has given *(Reads)*
Respected Rajendra Babu,
The 12 candidates out of 358 applicants who were selected to go to Japan for higher studies on government scholarship, among them is Rabindranath Samantaray, son of honourable Minister Debananda Samantaray. He who argues that he can not get government scholarship as he is a Minister's son, is devoid of conscience, because Sri Rabindranath is a meritorious student. He deserves this scholarship on his own merit. There are precedents in the past in this regard, as an honourable Minister's son of the previous government had been to America availing of such a scholarship. Hence your ministry is safe.

Second

Hearing that the Talapata river embankment is on the brink of collapse the Chief Minister, personally, rushed in his car. Reaching there after three hours the Chief Minister himself carried earth and poured on the embankment and seeing him do that thousands carried the earth and because of that the embankment didn't give way. Had there been no car the 50 year old CM would have taken three days to reach the spot by walk. And the embankment would have collapsed. Those who criticize that the ministers are riding motor cars are pardonable. Here also we have precedence – as all previous ministers were riding cars. Hence in this matter also you are safe – but I am sorry to say that you had said, after getting ministerships you will transform the country – but after three months I notice that the sky is the same blue, the hills are still grey and the grass is green. And the funniest thing is the government files have the same red tape – kindly turn the tapes black, at least this easy thing be done, you will uphold your prestige. Nothing more has happened in the last three months, therefore I don't write further .

Yours etc.
Sri Satyabadi Samal <i>(Matric Pass)</i></div>

An earth bearing coolie of the capital Area contractor.
(Acharjya was not disturbed after reading the letter – while tearing away the letter the backside caught his attention)

Acharjya: On this side also something is written *(reads)* "I know you will tear off the letter after reading. Yet I wrote…." Is there anything to comment on this Rajendra Babu ? *(while saying he tears the letter into pieces)*

Rajendra: I don't quite understand what purpose does he have in writing this letter. Again, he has given his full identity.

Acharjya: Individual freedom. Citizen's rights ! In a democracy he has the right to write to government, like this – may be this is what he wishes to convey.

Rajendra: A distinguished litterateur has said… "Our nation has the misfortune of being exited in our own inhabited land. In his own soil

	educated young man Satyabadi is a labourer under a foreign contractor – for this doesn't the fire of rebellion burn in his heart ? While writing this letter satirically along with his own discontent, may be for a moment – his nation's thoughts – his country's thought arose in his mind.
Acharjya:	May be – but he belongs to that class of patriots whose Inquilab – Jindabad slogan ends in the Jindabad of his self- interest. I know how to keep their mouths shut. I will reply to his letter.
Rajendra:	You will give ? What will you write ?
Acharjya:	*(smiling)* Are you asking this to Acharjya, Rajendra !
Rajendra:	Not one Rajendra – the whole state now looks at you questioningly for you understand what the questions mean. And you know where lies the answer.
	(Acharjya raised his eyebrows – simultaneously the old diplomatic smile played on his lips)
Acharjya:	Yes, Rajendra. Certainly Gita Devi is accompanying you ?
Rajendra:	Yes.
Acharjya:	Your passport and flight programme I'll do very soon – Ok then, let me come.
	(He goes – enters Gita)
Gita:	What are you thinking ?
Rajendra:	"A Government of the people, by the people and for the people shall never perish from the earth"

Act - I I: Scene – iv

(Inner block of Mandara Mohanty's house, Sita comes from inside. Looking to the front side once or twice, called somebody in signs – Immediately entered Makunda enthusiastically – dressed to go out to a new place – A bag in hand – full with useful things)

Makunda:	Did it work out ? Has he agreed ?
Sita:	At first thundered. Later after I pampered him he has….
Makunda:	Agreed ?
Sita:	Yes…
Makunda:	Did I not know that ! I never surrendered to you as the last resort for nothing. If you didn't put in a word Mohantia wouldn't have agreed to take me with him.
Sita:	Coming ! – You know Makunda, everything happens – but when my dues come up he starts whimpering. He says – I can't do such petty things; my shenanigans are there then everything is there.
Makunda:	What is that matter sister !
Sita:	I had requested for 2-4 acres of land – we did so much for them – he was coronoted – climbed the throne, if he wishes can he not arrange for two-four acres of land ? You are like my brother; when he hands over the list

	please remind him of my need.
Makunda:	This Radhu Pani, if he was not going, I would have got the land registered in your name.
Mandara:	Seba's mother *(from inside)*
Sita:	Going Makunda. You remember what I said. *(goes).*
Makunda:	*(There sits and examines the umbrella)* This umbrella at the end betrayed me – had it been of iron handle instead of bamboo *(Radhu Pani enters his clothes seen to be more than what he normally wore)* my.... *(pauses)*
Radhu:	My !!
Makunda:	My brother has come – look here; me too going Mohantia agreed...
Radhu:	*(Giving him the suitcase)* Here take it and hold it – you are lucky that you're going to minister with us. But be careful – the line in which we speak you will follow the same – no deviation – get it – otherwise *(Mandara enters with luggage).*
Radhu:	Take this, hold *(Makunda carries everything)* Go, go in advance – *(Makunda leaves)*
Mandara:	Come Radhu !
Radhu:	You saw the way the villagers were stubborn –
Mandara:	You saw how in one thunder they all became cold.
Radhu:	Yet if this time we return empty handed then our prestige will roll on the ground...
Mandara:	You be patient Radhu – you'll see how I get things done as per the list *(Sita enters)*
Sita:	Why are you so eager to go ?
Makunda:	How could I not go sister ? I have a family should I be just swept away without reaching

	a bank ! Acharjya, it seems is very powerful like Rabaneswara. With one line of the pen dismisses everything. What gall do I have ? How adamant I was, you know ? But finally, being twisted and turned I took shelter under the Quill Pen and surrendered to Radhu Pani – the time is such sister, one day even God held a donkey's foot. Otherwise is Radhu Pani a man ! Now he does not even speak of repaying my shop debt – let him not give. What to do – I'm in trouble.
Sita:	Yes, that thing Makunda – Bijoy wrote how he *(Mandara)* is respected there, held in esteem…. *(in slight low voice)* you know, outside he is neutral but in his heart …..
Makunda:	Do I not know that ? If there was no Mohanty no Quill Pen or stick pen.
Sita:	Since he is going to the minister, my dear husband has prepared a long list.
Makunda:	Shopping list ?
Sita:	O' no – Do you think this village will remain a village, there will be good roads. Tube wells will be set up on the village front. Minor school will be opened. In the jatra ground there will be a swing platform – Radhu Pani will be a contractor and my beau will be Parpanch – eh ! Let my mouth burn, what's that – Sarpanch, Sarpanch !!
Makunda:	O' great –
Sita:	And our village jatra party you know –
Makunda:	*(eagerly)* Yes…
Sita:	They won't do jatra anymore…
Makunda:	Then –

Sita:	Do thetara –
Makunda:	Wow ! earthshaking !
Mandara:	(*from inside*) Seba's mother !
Sita:	Anyhow you return by evening tomorrow, enquire about Bijoy – and ….
Mandara:	What ? Land ?
Sita:	Five acres will be enough –
Mandara:	Ok. I remember. Be ready with plough and bullocks by the time I come back. You have caught the hand of Mandara Mohanty, is it not ! Mandar Mohanty will plough the land? Rustic !!

■

Act - I I: Scene – v

(The lobby adjacent to the Chief Minister's office. Decorated with wooden furniture. Plain and neat. Mandar, Radhu and Makunda entered cautiously. They appeared to be waiting for some one else's instruction. The caretaker Satyabadi's voice was heard)

Satyabadi: *(from inside)* Please sit there.
Mandara: Sit Radhu, sit Makunda !
Radhu: Makunda – keep the suitcase and bed rolls under this bench. *(Makunda does that and they sit on the same bench)*
Makunda: Hey Radhu, in the village you call me Makunda but should you call me that here?
Radhu: So what ?
Makunda: Do you hear Sir ! If the Minister hears would he not assess our worth ?
Radhu: Don't be garrulous, sit.
Mandara: You see Radhu, how convenient things are ! We have come for audience therefore we have been given seats. Look up ! See how the electric fan is moving – on the door of this hall is written 'Waiting Hall'. If you wait here you can have the Minister's audience – how convenient ! There in that corner is written 'Drinking Water'. If you feel thirsty go there and drink.
Makunda: Who has written all these ?

Mandara:	The Minister must have got these written.
Makunda:	The Minister !
Radhu:	Hum.... Minister !! No Sir – such round hand ! ?
Makunda:	O' my gosh !
Mandara:	You see Radhu, what is written here ? You are requested to be quiet *(in sotto voce)* Hey ! None should shout. Sit quiet. *(All kept Quiet, as if there is apprehension in the air. Looking in one direction when Radhu asked Mandara, Mandara signed at him his ignorance. After a while Surama, Devananda's daughter, came there. Ignoring them she walked there, sat in a chair, glanced at them curiously. She was a mod woman and these looked at her in wide eyed wonder. Surama, perhaps, felt insulted, she rose all of a sudden and walked off fast)*
Makunda:	O' my gosh ! *(Immediately Radhu palmed his mouth shut. Surama stopped and returned)*
Surama:	What did you say ? *(All turned black, including Mandara Mohanty, black in fear. Surama just gave an incomprehensible smile and went away. Mandara Mohanty sat gravely. Radhu was about to beat Makunda. Makunda was almost on the verge of tears).*
Mandara:	*(Sotto voce)* Won't you learn some commonsense ? What's written there ? Sit with big people quietly.
Makunda:	The mouth will not open.... Then the land issue which Seba's mother had asked....

(*Again Radhu shut the mouth of Makunda with his palm. At the same time entered a gentleman – middle aged Indian, tastefully dressed. His name is Ismail Khan. As he didn't have beard or skull cap it was difficult to place him as a Muslim. He sat in a chair*).

Khan: Where from have you come ? Speak – from where ? (*All are quiet, only Mandara fidgeted. Before he started speaking, looked at the writing – Khan burst out laughing*).

Khan: Got it – Because it is written there none of you are talking. Since when are you quiet like this ?

Mandara: No Sir – we had nothing to talk about – yet after all it's government orders, why should anyone defy it ?

Khan: You are right; but if all orders of government we people had obeyed, then there wouldn't have been such writing here nor would you have been sitting here gagging your mouths.

Makunda: Then Sir, no harm in talking ?

Khan: (*Smiling*) I see you people are altogether innocent.

Makunda: (*To Radhu*) Do you see ? (*Radhu is embarrassed*).

Khan: Tell me where are you from ?

Mandara: Nandipur....Dist....

Khan: Nandipur, near Basta station ?

Makunda: Yes Sir ! Basta. If you get down at the station it will not be even two miles..

Khan: I understand.

Mandara: Your native place ?

Khan: I live in Calcutta – I'm a businessman.

Makunda:	What are you by caste Sir !
Khan:	I am a mussalman. My name is Ismail Khan. Is the harvest good in your area ?
Mandara:	You do business in paddy and rice ?
Khan:	Yes, I have come for that. Why have you come ? To see the Minister ?
Mandara:	Yes to meet him and tell him about our grievances.
Khan:	This time, perhaps, all of you have voted for Acharjya's United Party ?
Makunda:	Yes Sir, all have given – All….
Khan:	This is your state, you have cast your votes. This government has been formed but I believe, this government will not last long.
Radhu:	Why Sir ! Why do you say this ? Is there a more competent person than Acharjya, in the State ?
Khan:	I don't blame Acharjya or his government. Rather I have come to him to get my work done. I simply say that a superficial coalition of three divergent parties – how long will it last ?
	(Satyabadi enters – a young man of 22/23 in suits)
Satyabadi:	*(Seeing Khan)* Namaskar ! Why are you sitting here ? Please sit in the other room.
Khan:	Alright – Here I talk to these people – is the CM alone ?
Satyabadi:	No, honourable Samantaray is with him.
Khan:	Then it will be late I think –
Satyabadi:	Not for you – have you sent the card ?
Khan:	Here *(giving a card)* – their cards ?
Satyabadi:	What card do they have ? I have sent their

	names and address. You please sit in that room – let me send the card... *(goes..... Makunda was looking at him all the time as if known to him. Makunda followed him up to the door).*
Radhu:	*(To Makunda)* Hey..... *(Makunda comes back)*
Khan:	Did you go there to see what's in that room ? That's another waiting hall. But there the floor is covered with a carpet. On the carpet there are quite expensive chairs. If you sit there tea and cigarettes will be given .
Mandara:	From government ?
Khan:	Yes..
Makunda:	What ! free ?
Khan:	Yes, yes.... Free *(smiles)*
Makunda:	O' my gosh !
Khan:	What did you say ?
	(Before anyone spoke Satyabadi came – Makunda again observed him)
Satyabadi:	Sent the card.... *(Surama came again)* You haven't gone ?
Surama:	No, I was touring the departments in the Secretariat –
Satyabadi:	Come, I will introduce these people – Miss Surama Samantaray ! Honorable Debananda Samantaray's daughter – B.A. and Mr. Ismail Khan Managing Agent of the famous Ismail & Co. of Calcutta.
Khan:	B.A. you have passed. What will you do now ? Politics ?
Surama:	No, I have a passion for dance. For that I have thought of going to Madras. I know you; father was telling about you –

Khan:	Ok !
Surama:	*(To Satyabadi)* See – will you do me a favour ? – Father may be late. I can't stay anymore. I'll go with the car – please tell father – will you ?
Satyabadi:	Yes I will.
Surama:	Well then, let me go – Namaskar *(goes) (The buzzer rings from inside – Satyabadi also goes)*
Mandara:	Minister's daughter ?
Khan:	Yes Minister Samantaray's daughter.
Mandara:	She had come for some purpose –
Khan:	May be it was a pleasure trip with father. *(Satyabadi came again)*
Satyabadi:	Come, the call has come –
Radhu:	You understand Sir – this fellow is a traitor.
Mandar:	Who ? Ismail Khan ? *(Satyabadi and Khan went in)*
Radhu:	Yes –
Mandara:	Why ?
Radhu:	He has come here for business and there he speaks vile about government – traitor –
Makunda:	Ah you are all knowing –
Radhu:	Shut up –
Makunda:	Why shut up – see how he is flattered. He came after us but he is called first – and he is disloyal, traitor ! And you are very loyal. Waiting for long hours none bothers – What Sir ?
Mandara:	I can't digest the ways here Makunda – as if everything is illusory *(Satyabadi came)*
Radhu:	We are called ?
Satyabadi:	Not so soon – no – that Khan who went inside – know him ? Lakhpati !

The Quill Pen | 85

Mandara:	*(Lengthening his voice)* Y...e..s –
Satyabadi:	These people make the country dance around their finger tips.
Mandara:	Yes, yes, may be they are doing – who is before money ? *(to Satyabadi)* what service are you doing here ?
Satyabadi:	This – what you see !
Makunda:	Peskar ? Peskari job –
Radhu:	Shut up.
Mandara:	How far have you read ?
Satyabadi:	Passed Matric.
Mandara:	Salary ?
Satyabadi:	One fifty.
Mandara:	What ? One hundred and fifty rupees ?
Satyabadi:	Yes – one fifty.
Makunda:	My gosh...
Satyabadi:	What did you say ?
Radhu:	You unmannerly fool !
Mandara:	That fellow is just ignorant, please don't take his words to heart. *(Satyabadi calmly went away)*
Radhu:	You Makunda ! Has bile gone into your head ? You don't know what you say to whom. That man is close to the Minister.
Makunda:	I swear Radhu, my elder brother in-law who is a coolie Sardar with a contractor, under him this fellow was a coolie – I was there – I have seen with my eyes –
Mandar:	What cock and bull story you are telling Makunda ! He comes from a good family, educated.
Makunda:	There it was rumoured, being a Matric pass a lad is carrying earth – his name is Satia –

Radhu:	I tell you in earnest Makunda – go away from here, or else I'll crash your head. *(Satyabadi returns)*
Satyabadi:	Why are you shouting like this ? The CM is very busy now !
Mandara:	We can't see him ?
Satyabadi:	Why not ? If time permits.
Mandara:	But Khan went inside ?
Satyabadi:	Not only Khan, Singh, Bose, Ghose, Misra, Mohanty – many have seen him and many are waiting. Now it is late – to lay the Foundation Stone of the Secretariat Club House the CM will start –
Mandara:	What house ?
Satyabadi:	O' club house – where the clerks will play and relax –
Mandara:	You see Radhu ! How convenient. How the Minister is disposed off towards the clerks ?
Satyabadi:	These clerks and officers are the base. How will the administration run if you do not placate them ? *(The CM has risen may be he will go this way)* –
Mandara:	Who is the other man with him ?
Satyabadi:	Debanand Samantaray – the Minister ?
Radhu:	You see Sir – how many are running behind him !
Makunda:	Where ?
Radhu:	See here…
Makunda:	*(Seeing)* O' gosh !
Satyabadi:	Look here – he will take this Veranda. Stand here. If his eyes fall on you he may come *(All stood in silence waiting. Acharjya and Debanand came. These three bowed very respectfully)*

Acharjya:	Arre ! You people are here ! Since when are you here ? Come here straight from the train perhaps. But why did you not see me ? Satyabadi ! *(Satyabadi was about to say something)* No - No It was not right to keep them sitting here.
Debanand:	Where are they from ?
Acharjya:	Nandipur….
Debanand:	O' Rajendra Babu's constituency ! You people voted for Rajendra Babu – he has become a minister.
Mandara:	That's our great good fortune.
Acharjya:	You don't know this (*Mandara*) man. Very clever, done a lot for us.
Mandara:	What a lowly man am I Sir ! What have I done ?
Acharjya:	Really I am happy to see you people here. I want to meet all the brothers and sisters of my state, in their own homes. I'll know them, find out what they want. This man's *(Satyabadi's)* history perhaps you people do not know. Passing Matric he was working as a coolie with a contractor. When that fact was brought to my notice he has got a job here. *(While speaking this Satyabadi and Acharjya's eyes met ….. Mandara was standing near Acharjya. Radhu and Makunda were standing at a little distance)*
Makunda:	Did you hear Radhu – what was I telling – I saw him there.
Radhu:	Quiet –
Acharjya:	No – no – he has said the right thing – our principle is not to close our eyes to someone

	else's vile fate. Yes tell me Mohantia what news ?
Mandara:	We came for your audience, Sir – *(Acharjya was looking at his watch)*
Acharjya:	You said the opposite – we had your audience *(Mandara took out the necklace from his pocket and showed it – Acharjya picked it up)* This necklace ....?
Mandara:	*(Pausingly)* Se...ba...ti.
Acharjya:	O' your daughter Sebati – a nice girl – for us she has done dedicated work.
Mandara:	She says she can sacrifice herself for the United Party –
Acharjya:	Really – I haven't seen a girl like her in the rural areas... O' then, she has given this necklace – why ? *(Mandara was unable to speak)*
Debanand:	May be donation to our party –
Acharjya:	Is it true ! Sebati has donated this to our party *(Mandara smiled dryly)*. But why the poor child made such a sacrifice ? I had given her a flower garland – and in exchange she has given this taking it out of her neck – the ideals of this village girl will keep our Party above. Satyabadi send this news to the papers today – that an unknown unheard of girl from a remote village has donated a necklace to our party. *(To Mandara)* you are lucky you have fathered such a girl. Tell Sebati, I don't have language to praise her patriotism. I am coming..
Mandara:	We had some grievances...
Radhu:	The list

The Quill Pen | 89

Acharjya:	What list –
Mandara:	*(holding the list)* The wants and inconveniences of our side...
Acharjya:	Well – Make it convenient to come one day... I'll listen to everything. Today in the evening I have a lecture at the Rotary Club; at 12 in the night I'll go to Berhampur, tomorrow in the morning a lecture at Andhra Conference – evening –
Debanand:	My daughter's birth day – Tea party –
Acharjya:	The next day 23rd What's the programme Satyabadi?
Satyabadi:	The Chinese cultural mission is coming – the whole day you will be busy – evening there is dinner at Raj Bhavan.
Acharjya:	24th morning inauguration of expo – from 10 A.M. I have to be present at the cricket field – evening I'll host a dinner to cricket players. Perhaps I'm free on 25th, - no Satyabadi?
Satyabadi:	Sir.
Acharjya:	Ok – Come here on the 25th – we will meet here.
Mandara:	Huzoor! Please try to understand our situation. We are from long distance, how long can we wait here eating from our own hand and waiting – please just glance at this list – it will take a minute....
Acharjya:	I am helpless if you are so rigid Mohantia. You see how much work I have? Should I see those big things or your this list... you come on the 25th otherwise you have the S.D.O., D.M. in your area – meet them they

	will solve your problem. Will it do to run to me on these small issues ? Come Debanand Babu –
Makunda:	*(Fell flat at his feet)* Sir !!!
Acharjya:	What's this ! – Rise – now sit and tell me.
Makunda:	*(Rises)* Those who voted in the Quill Pen box, they did – and those who voted for the Umbrella box will they stay in this state or their home and hearth will fly away ?
Acharjya:	Who said this ? Who spreads such lies. *(to Makunda)* Don't you fear all are equal in our eyes –if anyone threatens you – see our Agent – he should explain those things to people.
Debanand:	Let's go. Driver !
Satyabadi:	Your vehicle is not there, Surama Devi has taken it.
Acharjya:	Come – you will go with me *(Both go)*
Satyabadi:	You too leave – the room will be closed.
Mandara:	Please see that our matters are also taken up – we are the have-nots – the hardhats –
Satyabadi:	There is no place for the have-nots here.
Radhu:	*(Angrily)* Why are you saying like this. We voted them to power – they could form government because of us and we don't have any place here ?
Satyabadi:	Don't lecture – listen to me. You have voted for these well – oiled darlings – here you saw none bothered about you. Only the smartly dressed people were attended to. Therefore I say, first of all be smart, then come here *(goes)*
Makunda:	O' my gosh !
Radhu:	These are all hypocrites – whose they eat,

Mandara:	theirs they sing – or what Sir ! Nothing Radhu – I simply think if you want to learn intelligence – come straight here…. You Radhu take this list, keep it –
Radhu:	We will see him on 25th !
Mandara:	Do you have money for the expenses of five days ?
Radhu:	*(to Makunda)* You had brought some money ?
Makunda:	I brought money to buy things for my shop, or to pay money to learn intelligence here ?
Mandara:	See what is written here, Radhu – *(reads)* "If you have any complaints, write and put it in this box".
Radhu:	Should we insert this list in this box ?
Mandara:	Nothing will come of it Radhu, after five years the vote box that will come, there we will put in our grievances. Come, they will close the room. *(Makunda by then was enthusiastically marching in the room)*
Radhu:	Makunda ! *(Makunda is marching the whole room in high spirits)*
Makunda:	What ?
Radhu:	Pick up the suitcase and bed roll *(Makunda glared at him)* what ! Why are you looking like an idiot – come on – pick up …
Makunda:	O' my gosh !
Radhu:	You won't ?
Makunda:	Hum Uthata nehin…. *(Held his bag and Mandar's bed roll, Radhu picked up his)*
Radhu:	Ok, you come to the village first ….
Makunda:	Come to the village – You promised the

	village people, you will float the village in ghee and honey and brought from the common fund of the village the ticket money….. come….. return to the village… You will have to plough the land of each one for two days – or else you have no respite. And you will threaten me !
Mandara:	Why do you hold my bed roll again Makunda ?
Makunda:	You are a neutral person. You have nothing to lose.
Mandara:	Alright let's go – tonight we have to spend somewhere – let's arrange that first. *(All leave)*

Act - I I: Scene – vi

(A city road – events following the previous day – Bijoy, Mandara, Radhu and Makunda enter – time evening)

Bijoy: It will be better if you stay tonight !
Mandara: Why waste money staying unnecessarily – we are here for last two days – there the house – family...
Makunda: Why not stay !! But sleeping is a torture – Yesterday after meeting the Minister, we had some food in a hotel and then slept on the veranda of the Dharmasala – but what mosquitoes....
Bijoy: You should have come to my house....
Mandara: You yourself are in difficulty, had we come, it would have been more weight on your burden.
Makunda: That room.... Is it not Radhu – where we waited for the Minister.... That room... had they left that room for our use.....
Radhu: Don't have dreams before sleep... this fellow will sleep in government house.... Idiot from somewhere !
Makunda: My gosh ! As if government belongs to him only !
Bijoy: He has said to see you on 25th.
Mandara: You please go for us – you kept the list ?
Bijoy: Yes, I have kept. But what will happen ? If

	from every village such lists come – what can government do ? Every day hundreds of letters come to the party office – give us land, house – pardon tax and water tax etc… withdraw sales tax…
Radhu:	Will these things happen ?
Bijoy:	Yes, ought to happen – but how so soon ?
Radhu:	If cannot be done – how could he promise to the voters during the election campaign ?
Bijoy:	All make tall promises….
Makunda:	*(To Radhu)* How could you give word to the people of our village ?
Radhu:	I did that on the strength of these people.
Makunda:	He too must have promised you on the strength of somebody else's words…. What do you know ! But you always talk big – what is that poltis, poltis – where is that now ?
Bijoy:	Whatever could have happened – the three parties which formed alliance during election are now falling apart, internally.
Makunda:	Yes they would crack up *(to Radhu)* why don't you look at your own house Radhu – you three brothers of the same mother's womb – you could not stay together – you parted ? *(Sashi came that way)*
Bijoy:	Sashi Babu – namaskar !
Sashi:	Namaskar, Namaskar … how are all of you together here ? Why did you come ? To see the circus ?
Radhu:	We are here for two days – we did not have the chance of meeting you.
Sashi:	I don't live here anymore – I stay in the same rural areas…

	(Thus far Mandar was looking at Sashi intently).
Bijoy	You are walking – what happened to your vehicle ?
Sashi:	The vehicle too is in the village.
Mandara:	Hey you Babu…
Sashi:	Yes, speak…. Speak *(Mohanty remembered there is Bijoy he couldn't speak about the necklace).*
Mandara:	You…. I was telling – won't you come to us again….
Sashi:	I am working that side only – hereafter we will meet regularly.
Bijoy:	*(To Sashi)* Where are you going this side ?
Sashi:	To Debanand Samantaray's residence – there is an invitation – on his daughter's birth day – you too must have been….
Bijoy:	Me ! No, there is no invitation.
Sashi:	Oh ! Well then, coming. Namaskar *(goes)*
Mandara:	What's he doing now-a-days ?
Bijoy:	Service – in a big company, a big job .
Makunda:	Did I not tell you – he was hopeful then – now he has got placement.
Mandara:	You too do some service Bijoy – if you work for the country none will bother about you.
Radhu:	Bijoy Babu is not interested that way otherwise as the Minister loves him…
Mandara:	What love is that ? I see here – invitation to Sashi Babu and Bijoy is ignored – what will you get from that affection ?
Makunda:	Yes Sir – What will you get from all that – you are a neutral man… let's go – we are delayed.

Mandara:	Ok you go Bijoy ….. Seba's mother has said – find time to make a round to our house – Ok go dear – go *(Bijoy bows and leaves)* come Radhu – we'll go.
Radhu:	We will go ? My legs don't move..
Mandara:	Why ?
Radhu:	The village people would be waiting for us. The moment we arrive they will surround us like hounds – what shall we do – say –
Makunda:	Sir is a neutral person – why drag him into this – you fend for yourself –
Radhu:	Oh ! He has become quite a spokesman –
Makunda:	Why shouldn't I be ? If the boat is on the car the car will be on the boat someday – Boy had come to become a contractor – go to the village – when the people holding your ears twist it again and again with wide eyes you will go looking like a fool – not a word will come out of the mouth – And you will be a contractor – no ! I tell you the Umbrella people were right –
Mandara:	What did they say !!
Makunda:	They said overnight none can change the country. Let people fight – government will be afraid – Only then our fates will change – And Sri, Sri Radhu Pani – was moving with a swelled chest saying – give your vote to Quill Pen and snore in the house – government will hang gold umbrella on your head – will lift you up a decorated elephant – now ride the elephant ! Come, it is late. (*All leave)*

Act - I I: Scene – vii

(The garden adjoining Minister Debanand Samantaray's Quarters – time, about 9 PM. Surama enters all dolled up- with her is Sashi. Surama is by nature impulsive – can't stay at one place)

Surama: No, no this is not done …. Very unjust….
Sashi: Unjust !! How unjust !! Why unjust ? In school, college, in women's club, on governor's farewell party you have danced countless times. You are so fond of dance that to fall asleep while dancing is your wish at times – which you have told me yourself – yet you want me to request you to dance for 2-4 minutes – unjust.
Surama: Do you have any idea about dance ?
Sashi: If I had that I wouldn't have….
Surama: Listen to me first. Can you tell me when to dance, why and where ?
Sashi: Yes in schools, colleges, Raj Bhavans, day and night – and I have heard in the harems of the Mogul Emperors – the whole day and night – 24 hours.
Surama: I'm telling that only….. Is this the Mogul Rule – the Chief Minister will sit here and I will dance ? What will he understand from my dance ? What praise will I get from him?

Sashi:	We don't need his praise. We need only a testimonial – you will go to Madras to learn dance ?
Surama:	Yes, I will.
Sashi:	You know how difficult it is to get admission there –
Surama:	I know.
Sashi:	But if you get a testimonial from Acharjya there won't be any difficulty. Do you know this ?
Surama:	Assume, I know.
Sashi:	For that you will dance.
Surama:	Then why a dance was not arranged during the Tea party ? Many people were there. They could have seen, Mr. Acharjya could have seen.
Sashi:	See Surama Devi – today is your birth day – everyone ate and rejoiced. What crime have I committeed that since evening up to 9 P.M. I am chasing you. I request you because your father had asked me to ! Why there was no dance and why it should be here, let him answer that. What do I have to do with that….. here for everything there is politics *(looking at a distance)*. Look here Surama Devi; Chief Minister and your father may perhaps come this side.
Surama:	Let them come.
Sashi:	But you go.
Surama:	I am to dance you said….
Sashi:	First of all let them come here – it is more difficult to make them agree to watch than make you agree to dance. You please go.

(Surama goes in – Acharjya and Debanand enter)

Acharjya: What news about Ismail Khan Sashi ? *(Sashi as if couldn't understand).* How was he disposed towards you ?
Sashi: Very good.
Acharjya: Where do you stay ? I mean your head office ?
Sashi: Basta Station.
Acharjya: When did you come here ?
Sashi: Yesterday.
Acharjya: When are you going back ?
Sashi: Tonight by mail.
Acharjya: Yes, Debanand Babu, please tell me ways of avoiding Tea parties and Dinner parties…
Debanand: Why ?
Acharjya: The Tea party is over but no one leaves because I'm not leaving. All want to have a chat with me – *(smiling)* A lady very sadly informed me about the break up of her daughter's marriage proposal. I don't understand how I can manage these social obligations along with my government's responsibility.
Sashi: *(To Debanand)* Surama Devi ..
Debanand: Where is Surama ? You know Surama is leaving for Madras to learn dance !
Acharjya: Yes, I've heard – When is she going ?
Debanand: This week – have you seen her dance ??
Acharjya: I ? Shall I see her dance ?
Debanand: Before going to Madras she wants to show you her dance….
Acharjya: Really ! But when do I have time ?

Sashi:	Today..... here....
Acharjya:	Here ?
Debanand:	You are her father – like, she begs for your blessings !
Acharjya:	Very well – let that be arranged. *(Sashi goes in)* Let sometime be spent like this – seeing the pile of files at home I'm afraid....

(The dance began and ended)

Acharjya:	Wonderful ! Surama has progressed so far, really, she must be thanked.
Sashi:	Will you please give her a testimonial –
Acharjya:	O' certainly.
Sashi:	Everyone came to attend Surama Devi's birth day – only Khan Saheb could not come.
Acharjya:	Khan Saheb ! O' Ismail Khan.....
Sashi:	Yes, poor fellow – suffering from gastric ulcers. He had hoped to seeing you here.
Acharjya:	Hum, Debanand Babu ! – That file of Ismail & Co ?
Debanand:	It's with me – you wanted my opinion.
Acharjya:	What's your suggestion ?
Debanand:	They wanted a licence for six months – my view is – let's give licence for three months.
Acharjya:	Hum ! There is a famine in Bengal.
Debanand:	As neighbouring state it is meet that we help Bengal. Bengal could be helped by this arrangement. Moreover....
Acharjya:	Moreover.........?

(Acharjya, Debanand and Sashi – exchanged glances and the answer was available. Acharjya walked to and fro in a slightly restless mood).

Debanand:	The order should be given soon in the file.

Acharjya:	Where's the file?
Debanand:	Here, in my house.
	(Acharjya moved faster- Debanand and Sashi were anxious to get the work done)
Debanand:	The order....
Acharjya:	If the file is in your house, how can I give orders? Bring it here....
Debanand:	Sashi Babu! *(Sashi goes in)*
Acharjya:	I hear, you are afraid of Secretaries? Because they are big officers?
Debanand:	No, no, why should I be afraid? Often they give very clumsy notes. Besides, they must be placated!
Acharjya:	If you want to placate them over and above their seventeen hundred salary sanction may be made for three hundred special pay; but what advice can I give you on this?
Debanand:	I heard – the 17 thousand rupees which you have approved of on that the Finance Secretary has objections – it seems there is no budgetary head to provide this amount.
Acharjya:	Tell him that he has no head! No head for the Budget? If there is no head, create a head. He should know – it is my order – it is Chief Minister's order and he has to obey it! You know regarding the file of this Ismail Khan, Food Secretary Patnaik....
Debanand:	Yes I know – for that the poor chap had to leave the capital and go to the Agency areas within two days....
	(Sashi brought the file and with it a Quill Pen and inkpot).
Acharjya:	What's this – Quill Pen?

Debanand:	After elections I don't write with any other pen except the Quill Pen.
Acharjya:	Is that so ?
Debanand:	Not me alone – in my house including my children and P.A. all use the Quill Pen.
Acharjya:	Bah ! A noble idea.... Holding this Quill Pen a sensation of victory runs through the veins. From this moment onwards I'll also use only this Quill Pen. *(Opens the file)* Had Rajendra been here could you say what would have happened to this file ?
Debanand:	May be nothing could have been done – He would not have agreed with this.
Acharjya:	But my order couldn't have been stopped. The way Rajendra has started playing with me from the beginning – it is he who had advised the Food Secretary; but he must understand that we haven't come here to be Arm chair Politicians – we've come to rule, the people are behind us. Why should we be afraid ? Should we learn from the bureaucrat Secretaries how to serve people? Ismail Company will get the licence – No one can stop it – Let Rajendra come back and see who is Acharjya...... and What Acharjya can do. *(Starts writing on the file).*

■

Act - III: Scene – i

(Mandara Mohanty's courtyard, time about 9.00PM. The cautious voice of Sashi was heard)

Sashi: (Outside) Anyone in the house ? Mohantia ? Mohantia…. (Sebati enters, lantern in hand – looks tired)
Sebati: Who's there ? Who calls…

(Sashi came stealthily. His face brightened seeing Sebati, although anxiety was on his face)

Sashi: Where is your father Sebati ? *(Sebati was almost hesitant to answer)* speak, where is he?
Sebati: Since noon has gone for rice. Hasn't come back yet.
Sashi: Your mother ?
Sebati: Asleep. Will you sit ?
Sashi: I came….. *(couldn't speak)*
Sebati: *(choked voice)* Sashi Babu…
Sashi: What happened Sebati ?
Sebati: Why this situation happened ?
Sashi: Situation ?
Sebati: A month ago rice and paddy floated here – now it is zero – people say government gave licence to a company – which company is that ? Why did government give licence to it? Paying higher price he has carried all rice – paddy to Bengal. We buyers, we starve as

	we don't get a grain. Famine is rushing on. The old man Sahu today died simply because he didn't get anything to eat.
Sashi:	You are so young Sebati….. You can't understand. The opposition is spreading a lie against Government to agitate people. Today paddy and rice are not available – may be tomorrow it will be available.
Sebati:	Where is it available ? To arrange food for one time father is running three times – even then he fails. Eating leaves how long would we survive ? Since Yesterday, not getting one bellyful rice mother in exhaustion has gone to sleep… You are a man of that company, you are the owner of that rice depot.
Sashi:	As I am the owner I came running hearing your plight. You don't worry Sebati, I will give you as much rice as you need.
Sebati:	You know, 21 families of our village are daily buyers – All of them are dying for a handful of rice….. during the vote they were told those who don't have land, it will be given to them….
Sashi:	But Sebati only for you…..
Sebati:	If you can arrange rice for 21 families I'll stand before you stretching my hands…. Otherwise…. They will die and we too will die… can you ?
Sashi:	Ok, I will make arrangements and let you know…. I'm coming *(goes)*.

■

Act - III: Scene – ii

(Nandipur Jatra grounds. The Dak Bunglow is afar. At the back of the stage a scenery of a Banyan tree – the first hour of the dark fortnight's night is almost gone. A starless cloudy sky – therefore it's doubly dark. The time of the scene is – a vast area here is under the grip of acute shortage of food. The voice of Makunda was heard from a distance)

Makunda:	B-o-u-li, O' Bouli.... Come.... Come... *(The voice came nearer – Makunda came on the stage – a pencil ray of light illumines only a part of his body – a long staff is in his hand)* Bouli O' Bouli..... where did the cow go – its late in the evening.... Bouli.... Come..... come.... Where..... had she been there she would have responded by her lowing. *(Just that time his eyes fell on a distant object)* What light is this – dim and flickering – *(calls)* who's coming – with light in hand who is coming ?
Radhu:	*(from afar)* Is it Makunda ?
Makunda:	Yes, yes.
Radhu:	I'm going. I... *(His voice appeared to be suddenly broken, he couldn't speak further).*
Makunda:	Who ? Well – was answering and suddenly stopped *(loudly)* who's coming ?.... *(after a while)* Who, Radhu Pani !

	(Radhu entered with lantern in hand, his health has declined, he came and stood taking Makunda's shoulder support) What happened Radhu ? *(Radhu despite efforts was unable to speak)*
Radhu:	*(In mild voice)* You take cloves – do you have?
Makunda:	*(Taking out from his waist)* Yes – take... put one in the mouth. Let the tongue be wet. *(Radhu after taking clove as if got back his capacity to speak)*
Radhu:	I fast walked such a distance – my throat got dry.
Makunda:	Where were you ?
Radhu:	At the depot.
Makunda:	Depot ! For rice ?
Radhu:	Yes.
Makunda:	What happened ?
Radhu:	*(Taking out a small packet from his pocket)* See, I went there with 100 rupees – whatever bribe five – ten I would have given – even if a kilo cost two rupees. I would have got five – ten kilos.
Makunda:	Didn't give ?
Radhu:	The gates are not opened. Surrounding the depot are police guards – all rice is being carried to Calcutta.
Makunda:	That Sashi Babu was there – why didn't you tell him.
Radhu:	That fellow is a fire eating hypocrite – where he hid couldn't see him.
Makunda:	What Rahu's shadow fell on the state, before your eyes in two months all paddy and rice disappeared –

Radhu:	Why should it disappear ? Go to the depot and see – heaped like mountain but sent to Calcutta.
Makunda:	They say there is famine in Bengal – Many from Medinapur have come crowding here. Young lasses are dying for rice – and in trains the police harasses them like anything. Oho ! the eye will not see. In Bengal it seems many died – about one lakh.
Radhu:	Famine is here ! – Famine ! Makunda ! Famine !
Makunda:	You have knowingly put yourself into difficulty – your paddy lasts the whole year.
Radhu:	I couldn't contain my greed. The trader raised the price – per bag twenty-five – thirty. Closing my eyes I allowed him to measure my paddy stock – greed for fistfuls of money.
Makunda:	O' gosh – fistfuls of money – now lick the money.
Radhu:	My legs don't support me, I have no strength to go home – the little ones used to eat thrice daily – now they don't get rice once in three days. After selling paddy at high price I thought if there is shortage, I will buy rice from the market. Unfortunately, people like me have sold their paddy out of greed. Now nowhere rice or paddy is available. How long will the children live on leaves and such things ? Can I not really save their lives ? They will die before my eyes ? Without food they will be emaciated like wicks and die ? Paddy was plentiful in my land – there is money in my box – will my children die in

this crisis !! (*Suddenly he holds the hand of Makunda*) Makunda ! You are my only hope Makunda – I am guilty before you – but my children are innocent – five guileless children – save them – you save them – if you do not look at them they will die like insects.

(*Makunda looked at him; his eyes fixed – he had tears in his eyes*)

Makunda: You remember Radhu – during the vote rally – here, on this Jatra ground you held my hand and said – Makunda do certainly put your vote in the Quill Pen box.... I said never....

Radhu: Today also you will say the same thing ? You will not put morsels of food in the mouths of my children ?

Makunda: Am I counted as a man ! When you sold your paddy measuring your granary ...... I had put a few straw bundles of paddy for my nine member family. Your roof and my roof touch each other, if a mustard cracks in your kitchen the smell comes to my doors. If your children will roll in hunger how can my children digest their food ? I may be ignorant, dull headed in your eyes but I do not like the idea –

Radhu: I'm a Brahmin by caste – yet I don't have the strength to bless you. This mid-night – Dharma is witness – He will do good to you.

Makunda: Ok you go home. I'll search for the cow and follow you. You won't be fearful of the....

Radhu: I was going to die – why be afraid of anyone? On the way I have already seen a corpse....

Makunda:	Well – you go....
	(They go in opposite directions – the stage is vacant – immediately Radhu screamed and returned – Makunda too came) What happened Radhu ?
Radhu:	Who is that – coming this way ?
	(Both wait in fear – after a while from the darkness emerged a skeletal figure. None would believe that he was a man. The entire body was skin and bones. Just a loin cloth around his waist – bearded and in his hand an earthen piece – he came dragging his feet) You see Makunda....
Makunda:	Who ? Who's he ?
	(The figure came a bit forward and saluted them – He couldn't speak despite efforts. Makunda taking Radhu's lantern went to see him)
Radhu:	Don't go near him –
Makunda:	He is a man – see brother how he is suffering – *(Makunda raised the wick and both saw the face and started in fear – the entire face was damaged beyond recognition)*
	O' the face is smashed. Hey are you Sapana or ?
Sapana:	*(Nodded his head – couldn't speak except grunting)*
Radhu:	Which Sapana ?
Makunda:	Sapana Bauri of our village !
Radhu:	His wife died in epidemic –
Makunda:	Father and son had no obsequies – went away somewhere due to acute hunger and famine condition. The son came three days ago –

| | where was Sapana ? He can't speak – hey ! What are you holding – a few grains of dry rice…. Eat…. Eat. ….
(Sapana made serious efforts to eat but couldn't)
Poor chap cannot eat taking rice to the mouth – who has given him this punishment? |
|---|---|
| Radhu: | I enticed him in many ways during vote – land will be given – house will be given. |
| Makunda: | What will you get from that ? Tell me how to reach his house with him ? Otherwise, he will die somewhere here – hey Sapana – come, let's go to your house.
(He held him and Radhu showed the light in-front. After they go a flash light shone on the stage as if somebody was testing the grounds whether it's safe or not – Sashi entered with his torch light – some doubts in his mind. After sometime Sebati came like a machine driven creature. There was no expression in his face seeing Sashi. She greeted Sashi with Namaskar, placing the light on ground). |
| Sashi: | I knew Sebati, you would certainly come, but before seeing you with my eyes the mental faith was declining. |
| Sebati: | Give. |
| Sashi: | I have come this three mile distance only to give. Does anyone know you have come here? |
| Sebati: | I haven't informed anyone. |
| Sashi: | Thanks ! This dangerous lonely night, the audacity which you have shown to meet with |

	a man – this is like complex plot. Not possible to believe unless you experience it. Seeing you today I remember another young woman – Gouri of *Kedar Gouri* !
Sebati:	What are you talking about ?
Sashi:	Pardon me Sebati, I said that emotionally. Yes – in your village about 100 from 21 families are in want of paddy and rice ?
Sebati:	yes, about hundred.
Sashi:	*(Taking out a paper from his pocket)* Here is the permit – at least six months' ration is arranged. Send this to the depot tomorrow – the company truck will deliver the rice in your place. But none should get a hint that I am behind this. *(Looking at the permit Sebati's face brightened)*
Sebati:	We can not repay your help if we take seven births for it –
Sashi:	But Sebati – I can't wait for seven births –
Sebati:	By your kindness twenty one families will be saved from certain death. In my eyes you are not man, you are God himself –
Sashi:	*(Smiling)* Is God available so easily ? For that much sacrifice and much dedication is required – you haven't done even a bit !
Sebati:	Give me the permit. I'll go – the night thickens – give – *(Stretched her hand – Sashi took her hand in his grip)* What's this Babu !! *(Snatches the hand away)*
Sashi:	That day after the meeting, on this very ground, I had said – you have life – you have heart. But what I had caught at first glimpse,

	I never had any chance to speak out…..
	(Eyeing the breasts of Sebati lustfully) I don't know Sebati –is it my eye's illusion or the fault lies with your wild youth. 1 can't forget…… no I can't forget you Sebati – this past six months you have burnt me in agony…..
Sebati:	Fie, fie – Sashi Babu – I am from a good family. Trusting you I came running in this lonely night due to extreme hunger…..
Sashi:	The same condition is mine. I have come running to you with my six long months' hungry life. I have made arrangements to save hundred lives….. you will not look back on this one life ?
Sebati:	Is this your last word ?
Sashi:	My greed to stand like this near you is so much that so soon I can not think of my last word –
Sebati:	You go…. Go away. Once I had said I am prepared to sacrifice my life for you…. But today –
Sashi:	You are not able to give up your love of this body of yours ?
Sebati:	You go – go !! Thousands die in this famine, if another hundred die….
Sashi:	Let them die. But Sebati however mean or lowly you call it none can walk a step without 'give' and 'take' ! I can't give you this permit without 'payment'. Ok, let what you say happen – thousands die – there some from your village will die – and die will be your father….. and mother….

Sebati:	O' how cruel you are – how heartless!
Sashi:	Minutes ago I was incarnation of Mercy – now I am cruel – why? You go Sebati – may be you will arrange from somewhere some rice for your parents….. (*started to leave*)
Sebati:	Give me the permit.
Sashi:	Sebati!
Sebati:	I agree to your proposal – give me the permit.
Sashi:	I give you another chance to think over it again.
Sebati:	I am doing retribution for the mistake I have done, beguiled by your words -
Sashi:	I have no time for your morals. Here is your permit – (*Took out the permit from his pocket and tied it at the Saree edge of Sebati*). I was imagining before coming here – listening to a few soft words from you I will roll myself at your feet, but you didn't make it happen. Unable to bear the fire of hunger man today, eats human flesh – that is my condition today. (*He pressed the two arms of Sebati – Sebati's eyes closed in fear*)
Sebati:	God! (*Sashi was advancing hungrily…. At that time, from behind a tree came out Makunda – raising his staff*)
Makunda:	Leave her – leave – I'll break your head. (*Sashi turned Sebati and took shelter behind her. In a second he took out his revolver and advanced towards Makunda*)
Sashi:	Be careful, throw away the staff….
Makunda:	Throw it? Who then will break your head?

Sashi:	Before that your own head would be in smithereens – you know what this is ? Revolver – gun !!
Makunda:	Gun ! You will shoot me ? Well ! Sebati you go – go I say !!
Sashi:	Don't go Sebati – if you go Makunda can't live. *(Sebati hesitated)* Makunda – speaking in earnest – throw the staff.
Makunda:	*(Shouted aloud)* Mohanti ho !
Sashi:	Hey…. I tell you for the last time – don't shout – and the staff *(He himself snatched the staff away from Makunda's hand)* Ok – now both of you move –
Makunda:	Where to ?
Sashi:	My car is on the road.
Sebati:	Sashi Babu ! You are giving us this punishment ?
Sashi:	Shut up –
Makunda:	Bone licking dog…
	(Without bother Sashi asked them to move. They moved and Sashi followed – At this moment all of a sudden Bijoy appeared there – in his hand a whip. He could assess the situation in a moment and immediately lashed at the revolver holding hand of Sashi – as a result the revolver accidentally fired but the gun fell down from his hand – when Sashi looked back Bijoy lashed at him with his whip. Despite this while Sashi was about to pick up the revolver Makunda struck him from behind – Bijoy picked up the gun)
Makunda:	*(Aloud)* Mohantia ho ! ….. come running…. Come running *(Sashi by force freed himself*

	from Makunda's grip but as Makunda picked up the staff to hit him, Bijoy intervened)
Bijoy:	Makunda – don't hit him –
Makunda:	You don't know Bijoy Babu –
Bijoy:	I know everything – please have patience for a while –
Sashi:	Bijoy Babu ! My revolver....
Bijoy:	What ? I'll return it to you ? *(Sashi tried to escape the scene)* Seeing this in my hand you still try to escape ?
Makunda:	I warn you – just stand there – if you move I'll make you lame !
	(Thus far Sebati was standing quietly)
Bijoy:	Sebati ! *(Sebati could not speak – simply cried holding the feet of Bijoy – This distracted Bijoy and Makunda and they became somewhat unmindful of the situation. Taking this opportunity when Sashi tried to run away he almost bumped into Rajendra Babu. With Rajendra Babu was the Chowkidar of the Dak Bunglow, lantern in hand. Seeing Rajendra in front of him Sashi's knees buckled. His hands automatically went up to salute Rajendra Babu)*
Sashi:	Y....o.....u !!
Rajendra:	But at this hour of the night what are you doing here ? Bijoy ...... Sebati ? Why is Sebati crying ? Why did the gun go off ?
	(After Rajendra entered Sebati stood up)
Makunda:	Namaskar ! You have come ! Put him on the stake Sir –
Rajendra:	What's the matter ? Sashi Babu, what has happened ?

Bijoy:	I'll tell you please listen. I heard this evening you have come to the Dak Bunglow. While going to meet you on the way I went to Sebati's house. – there I couldn't get Sebati – got this letter –
Rajendra:	What letter ? Who has written ?

Bijoy:	This Sashi Babu has written to Sebati *(Hands over the letter to Rajendra – Rajendra reads)* "Srimati Sevati Dei", At your lotus hand – The people of your village who are suffering in this famine, if for all of them rice is not arranged, you have written that you will not accept any help. Your patriotism has charmed me. Truly, you are the Joan of Arc of this country. Out of respect for you only I have arranged for 250 maunds of rice – but none should know about this beyond you and me. Tonight after 10 PM you come to the Jatra grounds and collect the permit from me. If you do not trust me, I am helpless. Destroy this letter after reading it.
	      Yours
	     well wisher.
	     Sashibhusan.
	Hum.... Sebati, you came here alone ?

Sebati:	Yes.
Rajendra:	Then, what happened ?
Makunda:	What happened after that how can I tell all that ! If by chance I had not come here Sebati would have gone from three almanacs. Mandar Mohanty's family would have been defamed.... Such times have come that this

	girl doesn't even get bellyful food. Enticing her with rice and bringing her here .... Fie, fie, fie. This fellow is such a criminal, such a sinner.... Sir at gun point he was taking me and Sebati from here !
Rajendra:	Sashi Babu ! All this is true ?
Sashi:	You all come with me to the depot, there you will hear.
Rajendra:	No. Speak here.
Sashi:	None have the authority to detain me here. *(Moved to go)*
Rajendra:	Stand there Sashi.
Makunda:	Sir, you just give way – I will make mushroom of his head. *(At this time from nearby the voices of Mandara Mohanty and Sita)*
Sita:	Seba – Seba where did you go O' Seba...
Mandara:	Makunda re – Makunda !
Makunda:	Here Sir – come here.... *(Mandara and Sita entered)*
Sebati:	Mother !
Sita:	*(hugging Sebati)* who brought you this way Seba ?
Makunda:	Sister, this fellow had bedevilled her. But she is your daughter – who can harm her ? You take her and go home .....
Mandara:	What happened to that letter Bijoy ? *(To Sashi).* Hey Babu – in the end you did this ? For this you gave her the gold chain ?
Sita:	I'll go, hang myself at his door. Why did he write letter to my daughter ?
Rajendra:	Please listen to me.
Mandara:	What's there to listen Sir ! You have come –

	see the whole thing – you have taken food from our mouths, dragged daughters and daughters-in-laws from the house – what else remains to be seen ? Speak – Answer.
Makunda:	If I speak you will dab me guilty. Why should he reply to your questions ? You are neutral....
Mandara:	*(Slapping both his checks himself)* Now, no neutral ! I was superficially neutral but in truth I was doing my machinations under that garb – Dharma did not tolerate – I now suffer my actions. Otherwise my daughter would not have come out of the house at midnight !!
Rajendra:	Listen – Sebati is not only sinless, but also admirable – the way she has sacrificed herself to save the villagers deserves the respect of the whole nation..... You please take her and go home.
Makunda:	Yes Sir ! Take Sebati and go home. We'll give him the right medicine...
Mandara:	Bijoy...
Bijoy:	You please go home with her, I'll go after some time.
	(Mandara, Sita and Sebati leave)
Rajendra:	What reply do you have for Mandara Mohanty's allegation, Sashi Babu ? One who is not getting two morsels of food two times how could you dream of romancing with her? You used food as an instrument to satisfy your lust ?
Makunda:	Speak Babu – You eat both times scented rice therefore your love is overflowing – she fasts

	the other time if she takes one time – what shall I speak ? I know since that vote rally – his passion is to grab others' property. *(To Rajendra)* Sir order me ! Let me finish my work..
Rajendra:	The police station is not far off Makunda, come, I'll personally hand him over to the police – yes, Bijoy !
Bijoy:	Two years ago when power was with the Ganasakti Party because of your instructions we had a strike in the college. At that time I had snatched away this whip from a police officer – today you are the rulers – what need we of the whip ? I had brought this to return it to you....
Rajendra:	From Switzerland I came to Calcutta – and from Calcutta I came here straight. I don't know Bijoy how this famine was possible ? Who's this ? *(Sapana came)*
Makunda:	He is Sapana, because of extreme hunger he went to this Sashi Babu's rice depot – see how he is defaced taking stone hits... Sapana, do you recognize this Babu – rice Babu !

(Sapana looked at Sashi – recognizing him he started attacking him with the broken piece of pitcher he was holding – but because of emotion he fell down and died after groaning for a few moments. All including Sashi sat by his side)

Sashi:	Sapana..... Sapana
Makunda:	Nah ! gone –
Rajendra:	Ours is a well watered, harvesting place – A green state, surplus state. Here people die falling here and there without a handful of

rice why ? No, no Bijoy ! Don't return this whip – if I can't at least with the help of this whip you will find out who is responsible for this ? Who is responsible.

■

Act - III: Scene – iii

(Road – A man enters singing – as if he is charged up by the deteriorating condition of the state)
(S O N G)
(The reception adjacent to Chief Minister Acharjay's office. A long table in the middle, chairs lined up on either side of the table. A flower vase on the table – some newspapers – two files and an inkpot. A Quill pen and some paper weights. The scene begins with Acharjya and Debanand. For some reason Acharjya is more agitated than worried)

Acharjya: None can tolerate this – no government, no government of any civilized country can allow such torture.

Debanand: We shouldn't have called the two student leaders for mutual compromise – that was a mistake.

Acharjya: Not only that – it was a mistake to acknowledge them as leaders. Two milk cheeked boys of eighteen or nineteen – they can't have the intelligence of organizing such a massive strike. We knew that yet we called them here to placate them – now we suffer the consequences.
(Outside the sound of a car. Debanand rose to see)
Who has come ? Rajendra ?

Debanand: No another platoon of military police !!

Acharjya:	What's going on ? Students will gherao the college there and armed police will guard us here ? No – I will go there myself.
Debanand:	No ! It's not proper for you to go there. They are agitated.
Acharjya:	Damn it ! If I can't control a group of students.
Debanand:	You don't have students alone – there are outsiders also – moreover they haven't forgotten the disappearance of rice and paddy !
Acharjya:	Why there is no dearth of rice anymore: It's plentifully available –
Debanand:	But do you think people have overcome the shock so soon ? Besides, why will you go there ? The Principal of the college is there...
Acharjya:	What can the Principal do ? He has closed the doors and windows and has shut himself safely in the office.
Debanand:	District Magistrate, S.P !
Acharjya:	DM, SP, IG – are all there. But what are they doing there ? A handful of boys will attack the College for five hours – and they will stand and watch the fun ! They are all out of their minds.
Debanand:	Don't be restless like that.
Acharjya:	But how could I be patient. Who is thinking of that ? Who makes efforts for that ?
Debanand:	That would be automatic. (Rajendra enters)
Acharjya:	Rajendra – where from have you come ?
Rajendra:	From the College.
Acharjya:	From College ? You were there then.

Rajendra:	I tried to telephone you from there – but couldn't. They have cut the line.
Acharjya:	What is the situation now ?
Rajendra:	They have left the college.
Acharjya:	All ?
Rajendra:	Yes.
Acharjya:	Thanks ! How did they go ?
Debanand:	Was there firing ?
Rajendra:	Yes.
Acharjya:	There was firing ? Why ? Who ordered ? Is anyone dead ?
Rajendra:	No – Police fired only to disperse them –
Acharjya:	Then, they left ?
Rajendra:	No – from their side Soda bottles and stones were rained – two constables and one S.I. have been injured.
Debanand:	This is the work of the goons. They were kept there by instigation !!
Rajendra:	May be ! But what's the way of identifying who is a goonda and who is a student in a crowd of five thousand.
Acharjya:	Then what happened ?
Rajendra:	Thereafter the police would have fired on the pelters – but
Acharjya:	But ?
Rajendra:	I stopped them – I called the students' representatives and declared that government will accept their demands and Prof. Mohanty will not be transferred from here – he will remain in this college !
Acharjya:	Then the students must have left shouting Inquilab Zindabad in satisfaction – the Police force must have sighed in relief – peace

	waves must have danced at College Square. – Traffic must have resumed on the roads – to convey this good news the newspaper editors must have been prompt..... But Rajendra Babu ....
Rajendra:	Please speak !
Acharjya:	You are a Cabinet Minister – you are in charge of the Department of Education – hence you have the authority to take this decision, but why didn't you take this decision eight days ago ? Why did I advise you not to accept the demands of the students. For eight days there was strike and today this problem – why ? Can you justify?
Rajendra:	I accept – this is a defeat of government from the point of view of administration. In other words from diplomatic perspective. What I have done, no one perhaps will appreciate; but at the root of all this is the pain of rice scarcity. In a few days – many have died of starvation – the stink of cadavers has not yet gone from the state – In this situation however cheap human life may be I didn't want to see the killing of a few other innocent students.
Acharjya:	But you can see the sight of people insulting me.
Debanand:	But why did you go there ? Those who had the responsibility of tackling the situation there, they would have managed it. We should not interfere with administration – *(Rajendra gave a stern look to Debanand – Satyabadi entered)*
Satyabadi:	Mr. Mohapatra and Mr Sharma !

Acharjya:	Have come to see me ?
Satyabadi:	Yes.
Acharjya:	Tell them – can't see me. *(Satyabadi was leaving)*
Rajendra:	Listen ! *(Satyabadi stopped)* *(to Acharjya)* Mr. Mohapatra at present is the Leader of Opposition – His…
Acharjya:	But what work does he have here now ?
Rajendra:	He has every right to discuss the affairs of the state, any time.
Acharjya:	Whether he has right as Leader of Opposition – he is your blood relation…
Rajendra:	Mr. Acharjya !!
Acharjya:	*(Indicated affirmatively – Satyabadi went outside – after a while Mr. Mohapatra and Mr. Sharma entered)* Please sit ! *(On one side of the table these three and on the other side the other two sat. After a while a bearer brought juice for them in a tray and placed before them. The conversation was on)*
Acharjya:	You people have won – then why did you come here ?
Mohapatra:	We have won !!
Acharjya:	When we have accepted the demands of the students ? ….
Sharma:	O' we understand – if this is our victory let's assume, we have come to express our gratitude –
Acharjya:	Speak – whatever you wish to speak.
Sharma:	A professor was transferred from college – this is a routine thing. The students demanded 'No this Professor cannot go from here' – this too is a routine thing. But

	this ordinary thing led to strike, firing, soda bottle and stone pelting and took an extraordinary turn – Do you know why ? The only reason is from the beginning government was visited by 'our ghosts' that is the ghosts of Mohapatra, Sharma and others. As a result the studies of students, the transfer of a Professor – all these vanished somewhere – what remained was government's sharp look although we know nothing about this –
Acharjya:	Of course because of our foolishness you people got a chance to speak like this.... Is it not Rajendra Babu !
Mohapatra:	Listen, Mr. Acharjya ! For the last five years in this very Reception room I have met you quite often – I have heard your allegations against us – But after you won this election I prayed – whether we do anything or not being in the opposition. Let not the misfortune of bringing allegations against you come to us – but you didn't allow that – whereas the false allegation against us is that we took the leadership of the students strike–
Debananda:	If no one's hand was there, the tender students wouldn't have dared to organize such a revolt.
Sharma:	Whether they would have dared or not you ask yourself. Who taught the cat to bite hands ? During the last five years you have in about twenty-five strikes used the students as cat's paw to drag out chestnuts

	out of the fire for you. Today the same paw is opposed to you. Whether the students have learnt anything from our leaders or not, they have learnt very well Inquilab Zindabad.
Acharjya:	Stop it please – If you have something else to speak – speak.
Mohapatra:	Such a great famine came to pass – but why the famine occurred – who is responsible for that? In spite of our repeated demands government have not informed the people.
Sharma:	And I have come to warn Rajendra Babu personally that the other day in the Assembly his party had challenged to fight the election on the Food Policy. A few days back – in the Nandipur Jatra grounds a great hero of the last elections, Mr. Sashibhusan has found a satisfactory solution to the Food Policy of the State. That's why, perhaps, Rajendra Babu is silent today.

(Rajendra leaves the Hall)

Acharjya:	The Assembly session starts after two days. Whatever you wish to speak, speak there. And you will get our reply there-
Sharma:	Today the students raided the college – and they had given notice to raid the Secretariat – who will give guarantee that they will not raid the Assembly within two days?
Mohapatra:	Before I leave I give you my commitment that in all people friendly policies of your government we will give you support in full vigour – But before that we require a satisfactory explanation from the

	government on the famine and the disturbances.
Acharjya:	If our explanation is not satisfactory !!
Sharma:	Then I'll request you to scrutinize your own functioning during the last five years.
Mohapatra:	When we had the government – you people always complained, this was not done, that was not done – but when the laws were made you first tried to break the law-
Acharjya:	Perhaps you want to say that your government was absolutely flawless.
Mohapatra:	No ! But whatever good we did, you tried ten times more to deviate us from the proper course –
Sharma:	But within six months of your forming the government so many accidents have happened – yet we haven't instigated or arrogated – we have been quiet without raising the ire of people. But if your explanation is not satisfactory, whether we will shout slogans like 'Inquilab Zindabad'. 'Acharjya Ministry be dissolved', give us food give us clothes else resign' in the nooks and corners – that advice we won't take from you !! We will meet in the Assembly – we are coming – Namaskar.

(They leave in a huff)

Debanand:	You just saw ! You now recognize Rajendra ? He got the credit from the students, - here while a discussion was going on he calmly walked away – thereby these people had the chance to speak all these. The day he married Mohapatra's daughter I knew he would

	cheat us – whereas from among the hundred and one numbers of our party, sixty are behind him !
Acharjya:	Sitting at my feet Rajendra learnt Politics – he can't cheat me so soon. Now it is 1 o'clock – before midnight today we must snatch away at least 50 members from the sixty that follow him – yes by ten PM tonight.
Debanand:	Will this be possible ?
Acharjya:	If this is not possible – you give up politics and go and cut grass. Will not be possible ? If 50 crores are spent for 50 members ? –
Debanand:	Fifty crores !
Acharjya:	Yes 50 crores. You go, the business must be completed tonight.
Debanand:	But where's the money ? Money is in Calcutta.
Acharjya:	At the time of danger you lose your mind. You complete your work by midnight I'll give you money by midday – go –
Debanand:	You –
Acharjya:	I'll wait here till you return. You go… *(Debanand leaves. The stage became dark – Acharjya was sitting in that darkness – the sound of instrumental music was playing in the background – In the background was heard a snatch of a song that was sung at Nandipur Jatra ground. A spotlight flashed on Acharjya's face and moved away – the background sound came as follows…)*
Makunda:	Thirst goes to water, how does water come to the thirsty ?

Mohapatra:	For this famine we want a satisfactory explanation.
Debanand:	I knew Rajendra would cheat us – *(A choric slogan on many issues)*
	(He was getting more and more agitated from time to time. The stage again became dark – from a distance was heard the strokes of midnight – by the last stroke the stage was lighted again – Acharjya was pacing the floor in agitation)
Acharjya:	*(Listening to foot steps)* Who's there ?
	(Rajendra entered – He appeared as if is on an important mission)
	You have come prepared Rajendra ! You are prepared to face the serious charges of the state and government ? Tell me: why did you go to the Raj Bhavan at 5 PM ? Why did you seek an audience with the Lat Sahib ? You are a Minister in my cabinet – without my permission how could you meet His Excellency the Governor ? By what authority ? Come on, speak up you Devil !!
	(Shook Rajendra's shoulders – Rajendra could never imagine that Acharjya could go that far – yet he controlled himself)
Rajendra:	Are you in your senses ?
Acharjya:	Don't you bully me – come on – speak up, Answer my queries !
Rajendra:	Why was Free Trade Licence given to Ismail & Co. ?
Acharjya:	It's the same old story ! Everyone in the state is asking this question – you too are asking the same question ! But doesn't government

The Quill Pen | **131**

	have the power to give licence to a man for doing business ?
Rajendra:	Yes, it has. But because of an open export licence Ismail & Co. raised the price of paddy and rice without any rhyme or reason – attracted by which the poor farmers released their stocks. Because of the open policy of commerce the Calcutta based company exported millions of bags of rice and paddy to Calcutta – the result was people here got nothing to eat and died in their thousands.
Acharjya:	O' to bring these charges against me you cut short your stay in Switzerland and came back to Odisha. You are a child Rajendra, just a child !! If people die in good number in an accident what can I do ?
Rajendra:	What you call an accident if I call it famine – a famine created and invited by you –
Acharjya:	You are a fool – a knave. I got your true identity from the students' agitation today.
Rajendra:	But much before that I could get your true identity.
Acharjya:	Hang it ! Answer my question – why did you meet the Governor – speak ?
Rajendra:	You have given licence to Ismail Khan to export rice to his heart's content and in turn he has given you a bribe of two rupees per bag.
Acharjya:	Rajendra !!!
Rajendra:	And in this business you have received crores of rupees from him – that money is deposited in a bank in Calcutta.
Acharjya:	Do you know Rajendra – you are speaking what to whom ?

Rajendra:	Then you say whatever I have said is a lie. Although I have all the proof I would like to hear from your lips that all my allegations are false – speak !!
Acharjya:	I don't know Rajendra – which malefic planets' influence has made you stand against me today ? I have brought money from Ismail Khan – is true.... But how can a fool like you will ever understand that this money I have brought to save the party – your interest also is involved here....
Rajendra:	It is a lie. To save yourself you are taking the name of the party. You always dreamt of becoming a crorepati – that's why spending 50 crores you wanted to buy 50 members against me.... Uniting three parties with different ideologies you wanted to break their unity by money power.
Acharjya:	Then you are.... *(was going out)*
Rajendra:	No point going out – all your efforts have backfired.
Acharjya:	What do you mean ?
Rajendra:	Ismail Khan's man was bringing money in a car – the money was to reach you by 12 midnight – but to your misfortune – Police have seized the motor, cash and everything. And Debanand too could not capture a single M.L.A. All members of the party are against you. In spite of all your evil efforts democracy in this country will stay – there is no doubt about it.
Acharjya:	Ra......je......ndra !! *(Picked up a paperweight from upon the table*

and threw it at Rajendra – Rajendra ducked and was saved – immediately entered Gita)

Rajendra: Gita ! Why did you come here ?

Gita: One whom I admired as God in human form how he has turned into an animal only by his hunger for power and pelf....

(Acharjya looked menacingly at Gita)

Acharjya: This girl, this hypocrite girl has snatched away Rajendra from me.

Rajendra: Gita – you go away.

Acharjya: Yes go away – go I say .... Go !

(While he was going to the door, Satyabadi came with a sealed envelope)

What's that ?

Satyabadi: Letter from Governor – came by special messenger.

Rajendra: A letter from Governor ?

Acharjya: *(Opening)* Governor's letter ! *(Reads – his face turns black)*

Dismissed ! I am dismissed ! I am a traitor, seditious traitor ! I have been dismissed...

(Shouting) No No No...... This can't be – I will not obey this order *(tears the letter)* Who's the Governor ? He can not dismiss me... I am people's representative – I have won the election – who can dismiss me ? Speak Rajendra speak, who can dismiss me ?

(Bends on the table due to great mental tension)

Rajendra: How greed for money destroys an extraordinary talent !

Acharjya: *(Rises in Anger)* Chaprasi – Orderlie – none here ? Satyabadi !

(Satyabadi entered)

134 | The Quill Pen

Satyabadi: There is a warrant –

Acharjya: Warrrant for arrest !! Who will arrest me *(laughs aloud)* S.P has come to arrest me !! *(again laughs)* I will arrest everybody – I'll arrest everybody. No power on earth can stop me. I'm Acharjya – I'm Chief Minister – where's my file – I'll issue orders.
(Taking a file adjusts the Quill Pen)
This bloody Quill Pen – not this *(throws it away)* Where's my pen ? Give me a pen. I'll give orders.

(At this time enters the S.P. Seeing him Acharjya's words stopped – and all his agitation was gone..... A black curtain as if was drawn on his face. He gave a pitiful look to Rajendra)

Rajendra: Mr. Acharjya !
(Except sighing heavily Acharjya had nothing else to speak)

Acharjya: *(to S.P.)* Come. *(S.P. and Acharjya walked away: Rajendra stood there – tears in his eyes – Gita advanced towards him. Rajendra wanted to speak something but could not. His eyes were fixed on the void. He wondered how to right the historical wrongs his revered leader has committed. That was the only thought in his mind)*

C U R T A I N

Gopal Chhotray (1916–2003) was born in Purunagarh village of Jagatsinghpur, a part of the erstwhile district of Cuttack, in Odisha, India. He is considered to be one of the chief architects of modern Odia theatre. He brought in significant changes in the morphology of Odia plays, both in theme and structure. He rescued them from the hold of opera and melodrama, and the overbearing influence of neighbouring Bengal. Gopal Chhotray dominated the Odia professional theatre for more than three decades. Beginning with Pheria (Come Back) in 1946, he wrote more than 15 original stage plays and 8 adaptations of eminent Odia novels, most of which were runaway success in professional stage. There were days, when both the professional theaters of Cuttack, holding daily shows, used to stage his plays concurrently.

Prafulla Kumar Mohanty is a celebrated literary critic, dramatist, Director of Odia and English plays, an actor, essayist, story teller, bilingual poet and orator par excellence. He has authored more than 25 books in Odia and English. The recipient of Central Sahitya Academy Award, Dr. Mohanty was a Professor of English and Principal Ravenshaw Autonomous College. He was also an administrator under Govt. of Odisha. He was also a member of the Press Council of India. He lives in Bhubaneswar with his family and writes in a weekly blog savimuse.blogspot.com

BLACK EAGLE BOOKS

www.blackeaglebooks.org
info@blackeaglebooks.org

Black Eagle Books, an independent publisher, was founded as a nonprofit organization in April, 2019. It is our mission to connect and engage the Indian diaspora and the world at large with the best of works of world literature published on a collaborative platform, with special emphasis on foregrounding Contemporary Classics and New Writing.

www.ingramcontent.com/pod-product-compliance
Lightning Source LLC
LaVergne TN
LVHW041639060526
838200LV00040B/1638